Dr. Albert L. Reyes

NEVER
ALONE

The Power of Family
to Inspire Hope

IRON
STREAM

Birmingham, Alabama

Never Alone

Iron Stream
An imprint of Iron Stream Media
100 Missionary Ridge
Birmingham, AL 35242
IronStreamMedia.com

Copyright © 2024 by Albert L. Reyes

Library of Congress Control Number: 2023946353

ISBN: 978-1-56309-684-6 (paperback)
ISBN: 978-1-56309-685-3 (ebook)

1 2 3 4 5—28 27 26 25 24

CONTENTS

PREFACE

This book is about family. This journey about family reflects my deep family roots, gratitude, and appreciation for all who have come before me. While "family" for some cultures points to a nuclear unit of father, mother, and a few children, my understanding of family is much broader and includes grandparents, parents, in-laws, uncles, aunts, and cousins—a panorama of linkage. I am intrigued and naturally connected to my family past, present, and future. These family connections cross cultures, nations, and geographic boundaries and frame who I am today and what I do. Therefore, I wish to acknowledge my family and dedicate this work to them.

I realize I am the product of several families who have impacted my life in multiple ways. The Stevenson family in Scotland and Mexico, the Garcia family in Mexico and Texas, and the Guerrero and Villanueva families in Mexico all contribute a maternal biological and familial stream of ancestry deposited in me and my family today. A rich history of Roman Catholic Christian faith and tradition flows toward me from the past. The Reyes and Rodriguez families of my father in Mexico and Texas form the other piece of my ancestral composition with a rich history of Baptist Christian faith. You have given me a place to call home and a family to belong to. My mother's eleven siblings and my father's eight siblings provided me seventy-four first cousins, with the children of my first cousins continuing to grow our family tree. I dedicate this writing project to you, my family.

My family story extends through marriage to Belinda R. Alvarado Reyes. Over the last forty-three years, you have been an incredible friend, wife, scholar, ministry partner, and mother to our three sons: Joshua, David, and Thomas. The family I have come to know and love through my marriage has blessed me and accepted me like a brother: Rogelio (Rocky) and Michelle and their adult children, Jacob and Rachel; and Robert and his daughter, ShyAnne. My late father-in-law, Rev. Baldemar J. Alvarado, and my mother-in-law, Elia Olivares Alvarado, accepted me as a son. The Alvarado and Olivares families have blessed me with a place to call home and a family to belong to. I dedicate this writing project to you, my family.

The families of my brothers form a tightly knit circle of belonging. Agustín (Gus) L. Reyes, his wife, Leticia, and their adult children: Andrea and her husband, Fabian, and their children; Gus II and his wife, Melissa, and their children; and Samuel and his wife, Jennifer Marie, and their children, all bring a profound sense of joy. Alfred L. Reyes and his adult children Ahnna, Caleb and his wife, Rachel, and Seth also fill my life with pride and joy.

Finally, my mother, Gloria Garcia Reyes, and my late father, Agustín (Gus) Reyes, laid a solid foundation of family and faith upon which to build our lives. I dedicate this writing project to you, my parents. Thank you for teaching us to follow the Lord wherever he leads.

Albert L. Reyes
Fall 2023

Introduction

A FUTURE WITHOUT A FAMILY

God sets the lonely in families.

—Psalm 68:6

Imagine a future without a family. What would it be like? You would never attend a family reunion. You would have no one to invite to your wedding. You would have no spouse to commit your life to. You would have no children, grandchildren, or great-grandchildren to enjoy. You would not gather with them for special holidays like Thanksgiving, Christmas, Easter, birthdays, and other special occasions.

You would have no names to write down for next of kin. You would have no one to contact in case of an emergency. You would not have grandparents, parents, brothers, sisters, aunts, uncles, or cousins to visit or connect with for any of life's experiences. No family would visit you in the hospital or attend your funeral. There would be nobody to mourn your death or remember all that you were, all that you did, all that you achieved. You would have no family to list in your last will and testament and no one to leave your belongings to. You would have no family members to serve as the executor of your estate.

You would have no need to trace your ancestry. You would be alone with no one. Your future would seem directionless since you have no family roots. You would have no sense of where you came from or where you were going. You would be alone at the center of your universe. Few things in life could be worse than having no family. What kind of future might you hope for without a family?

Edward Everett Hale, an American author, historian, and Unitarian minister, is best known for his story "The Man Without a Country," first published in *Atlantic Monthly*, in support of the Union during the Civil War. Hale was the grandnephew of Nathan Hale, an American war hero and spy during the Revolutionary War executed by the British for espionage. Edward Everett Hale graduated second in his class from Harvard Divinity School. In 1863, Hale wrote "The Man Without a Country" about American Army lieutenant Phillip Nolan, who renounced his country during a trial as an accomplice for treason and was sentenced to spend the rest of his life at sea aboard US Navy warships without news about the United States or the privilege of setting foot on native soil for the rest of his life. Nolan was reported as saying, "I wish I may never hear of the United States again!"[1] Nolan reportedly regretted his actions and was described as a man who "misses [his country] more than his friends or family, more than art or music or love or nature. Without it, he is nothing."[2] What are we without a country? What are we without a family? Who are we without a family?

In Mark 2:1–5, the writer provides a vignette of Jesus's healing ministry in the town of Capernaum. People heard that Jesus had come home, and they gathered around a house to hear him preach. Four men brought a paralytic young man to Jesus, and because there was no room to get to Jesus, they made an opening in the roof and lowered the young man down on a mat. When Jesus saw their faith, he said to the paralytic man, "Son, your sins are forgiven."

Leonard Sweet suggests the paralyzed young man had no hope for healing. Several men told this young man that there was no hope, except they knew of one man who could help him.[3] If the paralyzed young man could just get to him, it would be his only chance to be healed. Sweet emphasizes that the story makes no mention of the family or friends of the paralyzed young man. In the first century, it was customarily the responsibility of the family to take care of a disabled person. Sweet suggests this young man's family abandoned him. He may have been homeless. He had no family to support and take care of him. He did appear to have friends who supported him in place of his family. Jesus appears to heal the young man because of the faith of the men who brought the paralyzed man to him.

Sweet envisioned Jesus turning to the young man and saying the one word the young man never thought he would ever hear again from another human being in his life since he was abandoned, an orphan. Jesus said, "Son, your sins are forgiven." Sweet said the young man's sin did not cause this condition, but it was not the time to discuss theology. What was more important at that moment was this man's need for a family, the need for healing that included a link to his family who would care for him and the need for a place to belong. It was more important for the young man to know he had a father who loved him, accepted him, and cared for his well-being. Sweet asserts that this is the only time Jesus referred to another man as his son in all of scripture. Now the man was ready to go home. Jesus said, "Get up, take your mat and walk" (Mark 2:9). In other words, according to Sweet, "go back to the family who abandoned you and tell them what has happened to you."

The Need for Families in the Twenty-First Century

Do we really need families in the twenty-first century, or is this way of organizing societies outdated? A few researchers believe our society would be better off without a family, a traditional family, or family of any sort. Several voices have come to this conclusion. Twenty-first-century society has introduced a variety of familial relations that have begun to stretch the notion of family perhaps to a point of breaking and obsolescence.

Plato was one of the earliest voices advocating the disintegration of the family unit. He noted that "wives of our guardians are to be common, and their children are to be common, and no parent is to know his own child, nor any child his parent."[4] Plato further contends, "In an ideal state, men and women will not marry, but have the opportunity to procreate; the children will be cared for by nurses, and parents should be kept from recognizing their children."[5] In Plato's view, unity is the reason for commonality in everything. Unity is seen as the greatest good so that "they will not tear the city in pieces by differing about 'mine' and 'not mine.'"[6]

Throughout the centuries, others have joined the sentiment of Plato. Charles Fourier, Karl Marx, and Friedrich Engels were proponents of the dissolution of the traditional family.

> The Utopian Socialists Charles Fourier and Robert Owen had preceded Marx and Engels in their rejection of traditional family relationships, and many nineteenth-century leftists followed their cue. . . . Fourier . . . believed that monogamy was an institution contrary to human nature and was thus an impediment to human happiness. He also proposed that children be raised communally, so society would be one, big, harmonious family rather than fractured into competitive, squabbling family units.[7]

Marx and Engels wrote about the destruction, dissolution, and abolition of the family, yet Marx had a wife and family and maintained those relationships after he developed his views on the family. In his effort to abolish the family, Marx contradicted his own ideas by the existence and continuation of his own family. Even so, there have been some attempts at organizing society without families.

Families in the Nineteenth Century

In the first part of the nineteenth century, one hundred thousand people formed utopian communities to create "individual spiritual perfection within a harmonious society."[8] The Oneida Community was founded by John Humphrey Noyes in 1848 in Oneida, New York. The Perfectionist Movement came out of a Protestant revival known as the Second Great Awakening appealing to the second coming of Jesus Christ. The Oneida Community of New York was a Perfectionist communal society dedicated to living as one family and to sharing property, work, and love.[9] They called their ninety-three-thousand-square foot home the Mansion House. The community believed Jesus had already returned in AD 70, making it possible for them to bring about Jesus's millennial kingdom themselves and to be free of sin and to be perfect in this world, not just heaven. They believed in a system of free love known as complex marriage, where any member was free to have sex with any other member who consented. All men were thought to be linked in divine marriage to all the women; possessiveness and exclusive relationships were frowned upon. Children were raised communally and did not live with parents.

The Oneida Community ceased to exist over leadership succession plans, protests led by forty-seven clergymen, and charges of statutory rape. "In late June 1879, Noyes fled the Oneida Community Mansion House for Canada, never to return to the United States. . . . The community soon abandoned complex marriage and broke apart."[10] Despite philosophical and relational concerns about the family, these experiments were unable to survive or offer a viable alternative and could not endure the test of time.

Families in the Twentieth Century

In the twentieth century, American anthropologist Melford Spiro challenged the idea of the "nuclear family" as a universal principle. Spiro, founding chair of the Department of Anthropology, University of California, San Diego and born to Jewish immigrants from Eastern Europe, sought to raise an exception to this principle. He published an article, "Is the Family Universal?,"[11] challenging the work of G. P. Murdock, professor of anthropology at Yale University and the University of Pittsburgh. Murdock asserted that "the 'nuclear' family is also universal, and that typically it has four functions: sexual, economic, reproductive, and educational."[12] Spiro argued that the one exception to this principle was the Israeli *kibbutz*, an agricultural collective in Israel whose main features are communal rearing of children where the family as defined by Murdock does not exist. In this context, parents are replaced by couples who have children but are not identified with them for the purposes of raising them. The couples become formally married for the sake of the children since children born out of wedlock have no rights according to the Israeli law.[13] While Spiro challenged Murdock's assertion of the universal challenge principle of the "nuclear family," in his academic life, he remained married with two sons and several grandchildren until the time of his death.

Spiro's theory did not stand the test of time. Lee Cronk, professor of anthropology at Rutgers University, concluded that the attempt to house all children of *kibbutz* members together and to raise them collectively has not fared well. The issue of supervision of children by some women devolved into favoritism, rendering the *kibbutz* as an awkward system. Many who participated in a *kibbutz* have reconstituted their families, and the children's houses have become day care centers.[14] While the conversation as to the viability of the nuclear family continued, some researchers have concluded that the abolition of the family ultimately takes a toll on careers and children and leads to conflict and mixed emotions on parents and other adults.

Families and Education

A Manhattan private Episcopal school, Grace Church School in Noho, issued a twelve-page guide suggesting an alternative way to talk about families. The Grace Inclusive Language Guide recommended children use words like " 'grown-ups,' 'folks,' 'family' or 'guardians' as alternatives to 'mom,' 'dad,' and 'parents,' " as well as using "caregiver" in place of "nanny/babysitter."[15] This change was instituted to be more inclusive of the diversity of children and family structures. The guide also includes guidelines addressing various topics such as gender, families, sexual orientation, race and ethnicity, religion, and socioeconomics, including a glossary of terms and definitions. Words that are outdated are clearly listed to outline correct use for school-aged children. Some of the changes may have merit. However, recommendations presume language with no reference to mothers, fathers, brothers, sisters, and other terms used to describe traditional and historic family relationships are now normal or preferred.[16]

This is but one example of a societal disposition to leave the family behind. But where does this leave children and the important bonds of belonging? Children who have been adopted have a natural desire to search for their birth parents despite knowing that there may have been terrible reasons the child was placed for adoption. This is a driving force for most parents who place their children for adoption. Birth parents long to have completeness in creating a new family. Even in exceedingly difficult situations, parents try to create the best environment for children even though they do not always succeed.

Families for Children

Véronique Munoz-Dardé, professor of philosophy in the University College London Department of Philosophy and Mills

Adjunct Professor at the University of California, Berkley, examined the question of abolishing the family. She approached the question by considering whether the existence of the family ensures that the least advantaged members of society are better off than they would be with the family's abolition. She concluded that "the absence of full individualized legal protection with the family leaves the most vulnerable subject to abuse, coercion, and/or poverty." She argues that the family should replace political institutions that provide impartial care to a child with genuine affection and care of the family, thereby reducing the vulnerability of the worst off.[17] Even though the work of Professor Munoz-Dardé seems to have settled the issue of Murdock's proposal that the family is a universal principle, the effort to dissolve the nuclear family continues today.

If children, perhaps the most vulnerable people in society, are at risk of abuse, abandonment, and neglect as a matter of habit, how does this arrangement provide for the flourishing of societies in the future? If healthy families that provide genuine love and concern for their children are not the core of society, how will this shape our future?

Children in the First Century

A first-century Jewish rabbi had an encounter with children that was enshrined in sacred writings for the ages. Matthew, the Gospel writer, provides a front row seat to this fascinating exchange. "One day some parents brought their children to Jesus so he could lay his hands on them and pray for them. But the disciples scolded the parents for bothering him. But Jesus said, 'Let the children come to me. Don't stop them! For the kingdom of heaven belongs to those who are like these children.' And he placed his hands on their heads and blessed them before he left" (Matthew 19:13–15 NIV/LASB).

Jesus was on his way to Jerusalem, leaving Galilee for the last time, making his way toward a cross where he would lay down his life. Yet, he was not too busy to spend time with children. His disciples thought this was not a good use of his time since children were not considered important in the first century and the agenda of Jesus would not allow for a distraction like this. Jesus engaged the children, their parents, and his disciples in the context of having just taught about marriage and divorce (19:1–12). Jesus did not speak unfavorably about marriage; he only qualified the conditions upon which divorce is acceptable. He took the opportunity to bless the children by placing his hand on their heads. He honored the wishes of their parents, and he demonstrated how children can serve as role models for his disciples and anyone who wishes to enter the Kingdom of heaven.

What to Expect in This Book

The thrust of this book is to demonstrate how the family continues to be a foundational bedrock of human societies. The family is the sociological unit established from the beginning of humankind as an organizing structure for human life and the flourishing of societies.

These stories are descriptive more than they are prescriptive. Most of the families we will review needed redemption and healing. All families are messy, dysfunctional to some degree, and full of problems, even those in the Bible. Rather than gloss over family issues, my review of these family stories sets them in a constructive and creative light, focusing on solutions rather than problems. These families teach us much about what a family can be. In part 2, I provide prescriptions for healthy families. Chapter 12 chronicles the story of best practices at Buckner International after nearly one hundred fifty years of serving vulnerable children and families and how disrupting our best practices with one question changed a whole field of service. Chapter 13 recounts the amazing story of transitioning children from institutions to families in an international collaborative effort. It is God who sets the lonely in families.

In the following chapters of this book, you will read about dysfunctional families whose lives intersect with the narrative of God's redemptive work in humanity. The general pattern of God's mission in the world is to redeem all things, including families, to himself. Most of the families we will explore in the Bible are broken and in need of redemption. We will explore the redemptive work of God in the context of human failure, frailty, and weakness. Through the witness of scripture, we will explore how God works his redeeming plan through families. He still does today.

Part 1

Family Foundations

A Biblical Description of Family

Chapter 1

DESIGN FOR HUMANITY

The alternative to good design is always bad design.
There is no such thing as no design.

—Adam Judge, *The Little Black Book of Design*

L ife without a family does not seem practical or desirable, yet life with a family can be relationally challenging. Even healthy families have challenges. Families work best when they function according to their design. All designs begin with a question to answer or a problem to solve. The Designer of the family had a design in mind when the family unit was chosen as the organizing principle of humanity.

Author Adam Judge is right. There is no such thing as no design. Let's illustrate that principle with a few examples. I purchased my first personal computer while I was in the middle of doctoral seminars in the Doctor of Ministry in Missiology program at Southwestern Baptist Theological Seminary in the 1990s. I regularly produced twenty- to fifty-page research papers to keep up with assignments and needed to make the bold transition from a typewriter to a computer. The ability to correct a paragraph without retyping a page was a major innovation made available through word processing on my Macintosh computer. I appreciated the variety of fonts provided.

Even the creation of fonts incorporates a specific design and function. Have you ever wondered where the beautiful typography in your computer originated? At one point in the evolution from typewriters to computers, there was no expectation for the type to provide any variation from the standard letters. Today, a variety of fonts and sizes are standard features for all computers. Credit for this goes to Steve Jobs for introducing beautiful typographical design as a standard feature on the Mac computer, which led to that being the standard on all computers. Today, you will find a plethora of choices in the design and shape of the letters to choose from. But where did this idea come from in the life of Steve Jobs?

Steve Jobs stated in a commencement address at Stanford University that he noticed the gorgeous penmanship everywhere at Reed College, where he attended. "Consequently, he took a calligraphy class and learned the language of type." This awareness and fondness for calligraphy drove his passion for the design of the Macintosh. The question he began asking was, "What if computers could have beautiful typesetting as we do on paper?"[1] The answer to his question led to a proliferation of choices on most computer programs. The design started with a question, a problem to solve. The question of design seems foundational to anything that is aesthetically pleasing and, in some cases, takes lots of time to materialize.

Designing Gardens

The best designs take vison, time, energy, and investment to develop and maintain. The gardens of Versailles are an example of a design that took forty years to develop. In 1661 Louis XIV of France tasked André Le Nôtre with the restoration of Versailles' expansive gardens. Along with Le Nôtre, the king enlisted the very best engineers, architects, and artists, including Jean-Baptiste Colbert and Charles Le Brun. The king himself went to great lengths to review all the work down to the smallest detail.

Architect Jules Hardouin-Mansart, having been made First Architect to the King and Superintendent of Buildings, built the
Orangery and simplified the outlines of the Park, in particular
by modifying or opening up some of the groves. . . . To maintain
the design, the garden needed to be replanted approximately once
every 100 years. Louis XVI did so at the beginning of his reign,
and the undertaking was next carried out during the reign of
Napoleon III.[2]

The design for this incredible project took vision, time, and effort
to bring it to reality. If design impacting a computer and a garden
starts with a question and transforms itself into a vision that can
become reality with skill, resources, and time, what can be said of
the design of a whole community made up of families?

"A vision needs a visionary."[3] Every design needs a designer
who answers a question or solves a problem. The same was true for
Seaside Community, which was just a dream that started with one
man. Robert Davis was born in Birmingham, Alabama, and "inherited the family property from his grandfather J. S. Smolian in 1978"
at Seaside, Florida.[4] Smolian bought eighty acres of land at Seaside
in 1946 intending to build a camp for his employees. The plan never
materialized, but Smolian held on to the land and took his family
there every summer. Davis went to work immediately to transform
his grandfather's dream into reality. "Decades later, Seaside offers
a thriving town center with shopping and dining, all within walk-
able distances to homes, cottages, and offices. Consisting of more
than 300 homes, the community also offers an abundant assortment
of restaurants, shops, and galleries."[5] Seaside has been named the
"Best Beach on Earth" for families by *Travel + Leisure* magazine and
was listed as one of the "Top Ten Best Beach Towns in Florida" by
USA Today. Seaside also served as the primary filming location for
the classic movie *The Truman Show*, starring Jim Carrey.

"By design, Seaside has no private front lawns, and only native plants—no sod—are used in the yards. This plan makes for an environmentally friendly landscape, with no herbicides and pesticides, no underground irrigation systems, and no intrusive lawn mowers." It is a uniquely natural and environmentally safe community.[6] A visionary is someone with determination to advance an idea beyond its infancy, beyond a vision of what is possible. Davis was that visionary whose drive created the world's first New Urbanist town.

God's Design for Humanity

If people like Steve Jobs, King Louis XIV, and Robert Davis developed a vision for a computer, a palatial garden, and a community, respectively, who was the visionary for humanity? In the Judeo-Christian tradition, we perceive God as the creator and source of all things created and known. Therefore, the concept of design and order is intrinsic to God's character. Creation, order, and design all point to God as a source for what is to come in creation of humanity and the earth. It is fitting that we seek the origin of design for humanity within God the creator and designer. What was the design for humanity? How would humanity be organized for sustainability and prosperity capable of producing flourishing civilizations? Since there is no such thing as no design, what is the design for humanity? Who is the designer?

I look to Holy Scripture, reflecting a Judeo-Christian worldview, to discover both the designer and the design for the family. A survey of the Bible on the topic of family produced very interesting results. All the references to family in the Bible can be grouped into five overarching categories that speak to a design for humanity. Biblical references of the family suggest categories such as humanity organized by families, humanity resourced through families, humanity redeemed in families, human societies built through families, and finding life purpose through families. Families are made up of individuals, and yet individuals find their identity in the context of a family. The biblical text will define an individual as a member of a family, in most cases. Families shape individuals who learn, grow, and develop into mature and productive adults in the best-case scenario. Individuals are defined by their family of origin and are not intended to exist and live alone. This process emerges as a function of relationships within the family among father, mother, son, daughter, extended family, and social relationships in each community.

Organizing by Families

The Bible presents the family as the basic organizational unit of humanity. A sampling of these biblical references shows a pattern of organizing a whole nation by families. In Genesis, Abram is called by God to leave his father's household and go to a new country. God promised to bless all the peoples of the earth through Abram's family (Genesis 12:1–9). This same promise is conveyed to Jacob in a dream describing his descendants like the dust of the earth who will be blessed by God (28:14). During the Year of Jubilee, all Israelites were instructed to return to the land of their own family and to their clan to celebrate the cancellation of debts (Leviticus 25:10). The census record in the book of Numbers recounts the story of Moses leading the people of Israel through the desert and indicates organization by families. "So the Israelites did everything the Lord commanded Moses; that is the way they encamped under their standards, and that is the way they set out, each with his clan and family" (Numbers 2:34). The apostle Paul frames the family of God as people called by God's name in heaven and on earth (Ephesians 3:14–15). Over and over the Bible references peoples, clans, and tribes set into families as an organizational unit.

People organized into families, clans, and tribes have defined and recognized these groupings according to cultural and contextual principles. Historically, we organize into nuclear families and extended families that include grandparents, aunts and uncles, cousins, distant relatives, and additional relationships through marriage. In some cases, religious traditions include godparents and other social structures that define these organizational relationships. We find numerous places in Holy Scripture where the writer is careful to document the lineage and family of Cain, from Adam to Noah, the first nations, Esau, Jacob, the families and tribes in the Exodus, families assigned in the Promised Land, the families from Adam to Abraham, the sons of the nation of Israel, the sons of King David and the royal line of his family, the clans and tribes of Judah, and the tribes who gather to make David King, to name a few. Of course, this tradition is carried into the New Testament with the genealogy of Jesus.[7] God's people were organized by families, and they were resourced through families as well.

Resourcing Through Families

The biblical record also references individuals and groups of people receiving both provision and protection through families. This was God's plan to bless the first family and first siblings, Cain and Abel. Cain stepped outside of God's provision and protection when he took the life of his brother. Even after the first murder of the first sibling by his brother, God still found a way to bless the generations to follow. Cain transitioned from a farmer to a city-builder. Seth, the third son of Adam and Eve, carried the blessing God intended for the family. Much more will be said of this family in chapter 3.

God's design for provision and protection in families is present even when sibling rivalry develops. When the temptation came to Joseph's brothers to kill Joseph, Judah said to his brothers, "Come, let's sell him to the Ishmaelites and not lay our hands on him; after all, he is our brother, our own flesh and blood" (Genesis 37:27). While selling Joseph to slave owners was a terrible thing to do to their brother, they stopped short of taking his life. Years later, Joseph told the brothers who sold him into slavery that this was God's way to preserve them and save their lives (45:5). When Nehemiah led the task to rebuild the walls of Jerusalem, he charged his followers to "fight for your brothers, your sons and your daughters, your wives and your homes" (Nehemiah 4:14). There was a sense of protection within the family unit and the larger community.

Provision was another benefit of living in a family. This idea is also mentioned in the New Testament. Paul reminds the believers in the churches of the region of Galatia to "do good to all people, especially to those who belong to the family of believers" (Galatians 6:10). Paul instructed Pastor Timothy to care for widows and instructed grandchildren to take care of their own family to repay their parents as an act pleasing to God. He warns that if anyone "does not provide for his relatives, and especially for his immediate family, he has denied the faith and is worse than an unbeliever" (1 Timothy 5:8). Throughout the witness of Holy Scripture, the organization of humanity and the protection and provision of individuals are in families. God's work of redeeming individuals is often accomplished through families.

Redeeming Through Families

One of the most striking redemption stories of the Old Testament is the story of Ruth. Ruth's mother-in-law, Naomi, was married to Elimelech, who moved to the country of Moab due to a famine in Bethlehem. They had two sons, Mahlon and Kilion, who married Moabite women, one named Orpah and the other Ruth. After a period of ten years, Elimelech and his two sons died, leaving

Naomi a widow with her two daughters-in-law. Naomi encouraged her daughters-in-law to return to their families of origin. Orpah returned to her family, but Ruth chose to stay with Naomi.

The two women traveled to Bethlehem. A man in Bethlehem named Boaz was a relative of Naomi's deceased husband, Elimelech. Boaz acquired the land belonging to Naomi, Ruth's mother-in-law. He bought the land to preserve the name of Ruth's deceased husband, Mahlon, and according to tradition also acquired rights to marry Ruth. Boaz married Ruth, who bore him a child named Obed, who was the father of Jesse, the father of King David in the family of Perez. Jesus the Redeemer descended from the family of King David. It is through this family that God accomplishes his work of redemption through the birth, life, ministry, death, and resurrection of Jesus (Ruth 4:13–22).

Building Through Families

The primary way societies have built villages, towns, and cities has been through the growth and development of families. When Babylonian troops approached the gates of the city of Jerusalem, the people of Israel knew their future was in jeopardy. King Nebuchadnezzar captured the city and carried many nobles and city leaders into captivity in Babylon. The prophet Jeremiah, speaking to those carried into captivity, records perhaps the most important words in his book.

> This is what the LORD Almighty, the God of Israel, says to all those I carried into exile from Jerusalem to Babylon: "Build houses and settle down; plant gardens and eat what they produce. Marry and have sons and daughters; find wives for your sons and give your daughters in marriage, so that they too may have sons and daughters. Increase in number there; do not decrease. Also, seek

the peace and prosperity of the city to which I have carried you into exile. Pray to the LORD for it, because if it prospers, you too will prosper." (Jeremiah 29:4–7)

Even in a hostile environment and captivity under the hand of their enemies, God's people were instructed to build the city, seeking the peace and prosperity of the city but living normal lives, multiplying in numbers, and settling down. The design of the family is demonstrated here as a fundamental strategy to inhabit and grow a city to the point of peace and prosperity, to preserve and maintain the importance of identity and history as well as the unique contribution of each community in global history. Families are intended to create additional families and build additional communities who continue making contributions to humanity and continue the cycle set in motion by the Creator. Family is the means to human prosperity and purpose in this life.

Finding Purpose Through Families

What is the purpose of life for every individual, every human being on the planet? Is there a purposeful design in the creation of families that relates to life's purpose? When King David, the second king of Israel, was old, he made his son Solomon king over Israel. He also gathered all the leaders of Israel and the priests and Levites to assign them specific work and duties. Twenty-four thousand Levites were assigned the supervision of the temple; six thousand were assigned as officials and judges. Four thousand were assigned as gatekeepers, and another four thousand were assigned as worship and praise leaders with musical instruments. The families of Gershon, Kohath, Merari, and their descendants were counted as one family with one assignment (1 Chronicles 23:1–11).

As King David developed plans for the temple, he reflected on the instructions God gave him to not build the temple but to leave that assignment to his son Solomon. David said this about his assignment to the people of Israel:

> Yet the Lord, the God of Israel, chose me from my whole family to be king over Israel forever. He chose Judah as leader, and from the house of Judah he chose my family, and from my father's sons he was pleased to make me king over all Israel. Of all my sons—and the Lord has given me many—he has chosen my son Solomon to sit on the throne of the kingdom of the Lord over Israel. (1 Chronicles 28:4–5)

There seems to be a pattern in the Old Testament of assignments given to families for important tasks in God's work in the world. The same is true for individuals in families. God gifts individuals with skills for a specific life mission. Individuals are specifically suited for a life mission within the context of his or her family or clan. A life lived with a specific mission designed by God aligns with his overarching redemptive plan in human history.

Foundational Building Blocks

The Bible is full of examples of families as foundational building blocks of human society. Chapters 2 through 10 of this book will take a closer look at families in the Bible, even in dysfunction and disarray, to explore the place of families in human society. However, it is helpful at this point to consider non-biblical sources, nonreligious, and nontheological professionals who arrive at similar conclusions about the family reflected in the Bible.

Jim Denison's "Daily Article" featured a commentary on David Brooks's essay published in the *Atlantic Monthly* in January of 2020, "The Nuclear Family Was a Mistake." Denison summarized

Brooks's point that our culture has a hunger for authentic family. Denison concluded Brooks did a good job identifying the problem in the collapse of the nuclear family but also points out the opportunity available to the family of God to provide a solution through local churches willing to welcome people into a loving community.[8] While Brooks's critique and disappointment of the nuclear family accentuates a societal problem, he still points to the need for a family, a forged family of sorts. Many other nonreligious scholars and researchers have come to the same conclusion about the need for families in society as a foundational and organizational unit.

The Department for Children, Schools and Families in London published an article concluding that "strong families are the bedrock of our society. Families give children the love and security they need to grow up and explore the world, and the moral guidance and aspiration to make the most of their talents and be good citizens."[9] Contributing to a strategic plan for Family Service America, researchers Sviridoff and Ryan "embraced the idea that a healthy society is built on strong families and communities and not on families alone."[10] These secular researchers agree that families are critical to human flourishing. Another researcher introduced the concept of family as an essential to link individuals to the larger community. Laird asserted, "The family . . . provides the major context for individual growth and development and mediates between the individual and society. . . . The nuclear or intergenerational family occupied center stage in the various models, which fits society's emphasis on defining family in biological rather than social terms."[11] Families are viewed as an essential and undeniable structure for individuals in communities.

Numerous examples of published secular research point to the indispensable nature of a healthy family for the greater good of communities and societies. Several nonreligious books make the same claim. Suzanne Dixon wrote *The Roman Family*, published by Johns Hopkins University Press in 1992. Her book focused on the historical nature of first-century Roman culture. She notes the Latin word *familia* was used in ancient Rome and concluded, "Whatever variations there might be in the constitution and description of the family, it is a universal human institution, and the Romans were human. They unquestionably had families and saw the family as central to their personal lives and to society."[12] The concept of family is not a recent invention, rather, we have evidence this societal structure existed in the first century. Dixon further asserts, "The perception of the family as haven is often described by historians of the eighteenth and nineteenth centuries as a modern development; therefore, it is important to note that the same attitudes seem to have existed in Roman times, sometimes expressed in terms strikingly similar to the modern ones."[13]

Other nonreligious authors have affirmed Dixon's premise of the unquestionable need for families but have also commented on attempts to eliminate the need for families. Stevan Harrell, in *Human Families*, concluded, "Attempts to replace the family have failed, and the basic building blocks of semi-permanent pair bonding and parent-child links have reasserted themselves. There is thus little reason to think that in the future we will ever see the withering away of the family."[14] A growing body of nonreligious literature points to the family as a foundation bedrock structure for flourishing of societies.

Government agencies have come to the same conclusion. A report published by the Inter-American Commission on Human Rights on the rights of a child concluded that "the family is the natural and fundamental group unit of society and is entitled to protection by society and the State." In fact, "Article VI of the American Declaration [of the Rights and Duties of Man] expresses that notion in similar terms: 'Every person has the right to establish a family, the basic element of society, and to receive protection therefore.' "[15]

The Atlantic echoed international sentiment in their article, "The Nuclear Family Is Still Indispensable." The article states, "It turns out that the relationship between nuclear families and larger communities is more symbiotic than substitutionary, more nonnuclear forms of family life, research has yet to show that they are entirely equipped to shoulder the unique role of a child's two parents."[16] The article goes on to list the positive effects of stable marriage and stable nuclear families as well as the positive effect of these families on neighborhoods, towns, and cities as flourishing places when sustained by lots of married households. Harvard sociologist Robert Sampson is quoted in this article as saying, "Family structure is one of the strongest, if not the strongest, predictor of variations in urban violence across cities in the United States."[17] Wilcox and Boyd assert, "To be sure, the isolated nuclear family detached from all social support is simply not workable for most people. Married couples raising children, as well as other family forms, are more likely to thrive when they are embedded in strong networks of friends, family, community, and religious congregations."[18] Essentially, authors, researchers, and social service experts all agree on the foundational nature and impact of healthy families for the flourishing of communities and societies as a universal principle.

The Positive Power of a Family

Much of the literature on the efficacy of the nuclear family is written from an American perspective but also has universal appeal. Kurt Jefferson, Dean of Graduate Studies at Spalding University, published "The American Family: The Stabilizing Factor in a Changing Society," and commented on the viability and universality of the nuclear family. He said, "The family has been widely perceived to be the foundational unit of organization for most societies. The fact that the family is often taken for granted in most historical descriptions of society allows us to realize that the concept of family has remained fairly stable for centuries in both non-Western and Western civilizations."[19]

Oxford University Press published *The Family in Christian Social and Political Thought* by Brent Waters. In this volume, he examines the historical roots and contemporary implications of the virtual disappearance of the family in the late liberal and Christian social and political thought. He asserts the teaching of Jesus against the family and Paul's indifference toward marriage and family, as well as the New Testament's household codes against the backdrop of the Greco-Roman emphasis on the family as the fundamental social cell.

Jesus, however, did not forbid marriage or condemn familial ties. In fact, he commended marriage in prohibiting divorce. He taught that familial bonds are condemned only when they prevent wholehearted loyalty to the kingdom of God.[20] Waters concludes that although structure of the family has changed over time, there are nonetheless some continuous strands that may inform present-day deliberation. He asserts, "When the normative ordering of familial affinities is ignored or discounted, then other institutions become distorted in attempting to fill the void by assuming roles they are ill-equipped to perform. A school, for example, is not suited for assuming the primary responsibility of childrearing."[21]

Overall, the literature on the family indicates that the family unit is foundational to human society and appears to have overcome efforts to replace it with a substitute. The family appears to have stood the test of time. The design of the family continues to endure even in its changing forms.

The notion of design for all things helps us think about effective change for humanity through families. The Bible serves as a written record of how families form the foundational and organizational foundation of human societies. Even nonreligious sources agree that families represent the best structure for the flourishing of human societies. While there have been attempts to deconstruct and replace the family, none of these attempts have been successful. The family remains the foundational bedrock of human society, even with its challenges and imperfections.

The family is the Designer's plan for humanity. What examples of family do we have in sacred literature to help us understand how families work? We must look beyond ourselves to find the answers to these questions.

Questions for Reflection

1. What is your reaction to the notion that there is a design for families?
2. What is the purpose of families today?
3. Do you believe we need families for the flourishing of humanity?
4. How does your church encourage the family unit through its programming?
5. Where do families go for help in your community?
6. How would you envision the concept of family in God's core identity?

Chapter 2

THE DIVINE FAMILY

Father, Son, and Spirit

> The family, which originates in the love of man and woman,
> ultimately derives from the mystery of God.
>
> —Pope John Paul II

When God, the creator, formed the first man and woman, he decided to organize humanity in the form of a family. Are there any precedents to the family prior to creation?

To understand the origin and meaning of family, we must start with the identity of God, the designer of family. Before the first human family came to being, the Divine Family existed, so we must dive into the mystery of God to learn about the family. The focus on the Divine Family is a mystery, something that is difficult or impossible to understand or explain. Pope John Paul II was exactly right. This journey may not bring a full understanding of God as triune, but it will lead toward an apprehension of the concept even if our comprehension is limited. There are many things in life we do not understand, yet we accept them as fact, truth, and real. While we may understand how the sun knows when and where to rise, the moon knows when to hide, and the clouds know how to gather to produce rain, we are hard-pressed to know why. The Bible is a good place to search for answers to these questions, to look for insights, and to draw conclusions from what this ancient text tells us about God the Father, God the Son, God the Spirit and how they are related. The Christian tradition refers to this three-person God as the Trinity. This chapter will look to the biblical text to guide us in the exploration of God as three persons in one and how this relates to human families.

Family Before Humanity

The first known reference to family precedes humanity because the Judeo-Christian tradition contends for the existence of God prior to the first human being. The first reference to a plurality of individuals or beings in human literature is found in the first book of the Bible, in Genesis 1:26–27: "Then God said, 'Let us make man in our image, in our likeness, and let them rule over the fish of the sea and the birds of the air, over the livestock, over all the earth, and over all the creatures that move along the ground.' So God created man in his own image, in the image of God he created him; male and female he created them."

Where did the idea of family come from? A few principles stand out from this reference describing the creation of humanity. God has a voice. He spoke creation into being. What kind of voice has the power to speak something into being? It is God's voice, a supernatural voice, his own words causing something to come into being. When God spoke about creating the first humans, he identified himself in the plural form with "Let us." We know from God's voice there was more than one entity or individual present for the action of creation. The plural God said the creation was to carry an image and likeness reflecting a plural identity when God referred to "our image, our like-ness." Both male and female humans carried the image and likeness of God, a plural supernatural being. We know from this text that God is the head source of human life. He is the origin. This is the first reference to God as a plural being in the Old Testament.

The people of Israel who followed God out of Egypt and into the desert for forty years grew impatient about following a God they could not see. Their Egyptian captors had gods that could be seen: Amun-Ra, the hidden god; Mut, the mother goddess; Osiris, the god of the dead; Anubis, the divine embalmer; and Ra, the god of the sun and radiance. Yet the Israelites had no way of seeing God. Despite seeing the way God worked to free the Israelites from slavery through the plagues (Exodus 7–11), the parting of the Red Sea (13–14), the provision of food in the desert and water from a rock (16–17), they demanded to see God.

Moses went up to the mountain to receive the Law of God. The people waited below and grew impatient. They lost track of Moses and petitioned Aaron, another leader, to fashion a god made in the image of a calf to go before them in their journey to the Promised Land. The people wanted a god they could see. Aaron instructed them to contribute the gold they had, and he fashioned an idol made from it.

The people of Israel gathered in the desert and clearly violated the first Law of God: to have no other gods before him. When Moses returned from the mountain with two tablets and the Law of God written on them, he became very angry and destroyed the tablets, burned the golden calf, ground it into dust, mixed the dust with water, and made the Israelites drink it (Exodus 32). After Moses pointed out the sin of the people, he offered to return to the mountain to atone for their sins. The people of Israel continued to rebel against God, and a whole generation of slaves were unable to cross over into the Promised Land because of their sin. This pattern continued over hundreds of years until God provided a savior in his Son.

New Testament Reference to the Trinitarian Family

What does the New Testament say about God in the plural? A unique reference to a plural God at creation is found in the apostle Paul's letter to the church at Colossae. In his reference to Jesus, Paul writes,

> He is the image of the invisible God, the firstborn over all creation. For by him all things were created: things in heaven and on earth, visible and invisible, whether thrones or powers or rulers or authorities; all things were created by him and for him. He is before all things, and in him all things hold together. And he is the head of the body, the church; he is the beginning and the firstborn from among the dead, so that in everything he might have the supremacy. For God was pleased to have all his fullness dwell in him, and through him to reconcile to himself all things, whether things on earth or things in heaven, by making peace through his blood, shed on the cross. (Colossians 1:15–20)

Most commentators assert that this passage of scripture is a fragment of a hymn used by the early church, especially in Asia Minor.[1] David Garland suggests this hymn fragment, a piece of majestic poetry, was to be read as part of the worship experience in the early church.[2] Barker contends this poetic hymn was the apostle Paul's answer to heretical teaching in the church at Colossae.[3] Even in contemporary preaching, preachers use a poem, a song, or a hymn as an integrated part of the sermon.

This passage of scripture points to the Trinity at creation and establishes Jesus Christ, a first-century Jewish rabbi, as the visible image of the invisible God. The Old Testament God was invisible, but God in the New Testament became visible in the person of Jesus Christ, the Son of God. Melick reports the word for image is *eikon* in New Testament Greek, *icon* in English.[4] An icon bears the image of something so that one has an idea of what that something is. However, Garland contends the icon in Paul's letter to the Colossians indicates Jesus as the exact representation of God. He argues that while all humans are made in the image of God, pointing back to the Genesis account, Jesus is the only "satisfactory image of God."[5] McKnight agrees with Garland saying while all humans are an icon of God, Jesus is the only true icon of God.[6] Beale calls Paul's reference to Jesus as "Jesus imaging," an exact representation of God in human form, and sees Jesus as the agent of creation.[7] In other words, the plural God in the New Testament identifies Jesus as one of its members. He is an active agent in creation. Melick says God is the architect in creation while Jesus is the implementer who brings creation into existence.[8]

In the passage above, Paul contends all things in creation are made by, in, and for Jesus Christ. He also posits Jesus as the one who holds all creation together. He is not only the creator but also the sustainer of all we know as creation. Hay asserts that the hymn gives its most direct statements about the relationship between Jesus Christ the Son and God the Father.[9] Jesus Christ, the Son of God, and God the Father form the first two persons of the plural God according to the record in Genesis and Colossians. God the Father is another person in this Divine Family, and there is one more to make them three in one, the Trinity.

The Trinitarian Family

How do we describe this plural God as three in one, as Trinity? Let's start with Jesus, a member of the plural God, and consider his reference to God as Father. When Jesus taught his disciples to pray, he said pray like this: "Our Father in heaven, hallowed be your name, your kingdom come, your will be done on earth as it is in heaven" (Matthew 6:9–10). The whole prayer is to God, who is the Father in heaven who forgives, leads, and delivers. Jesus modeled reference to God as Father when he was on the cross between two thieves. "Jesus said, 'Father, forgive them, for they do not know what they are doing'" (Luke 23:34).

The Gospel of John has several references to God as Father from Jesus's perspective. When Jewish people confronted Jesus about his teaching and reference to God as Father, Jesus said to them, "No one can come to me unless the Father who sent me draws him, and I will raise him up at the last day" (John 6:44). Jesus was describing an intimate father-son relationship with God the Father. He also said, "Everyone who listens to the Father and learns from him comes to me. No one has seen the Father except the one who is from God" (John 6:45–46). There is no doubt Jesus was clear on the point of God being not only *a* father but *his* Father.

This is the same God the Father present at creation, the source and origin of human life. He is a loving, heavenly Father. At the baptism of Jesus, the Gospel of Matthew records a voice coming down from heaven saying, "This is my Son, whom I love; with him I am well pleased" (Matthew 3:17). We can clearly see the love of the Father for the Son. This kind of love is seen in human families as well but not limited to fathers and sons. Familial love exists between mother and sons, fathers and daughters, father and mother, sisters and brothers.

Another relationship Jesus used was a metaphor of a shepherd and his sheep. Jesus said, "I am the good shepherd. The good shepherd lays down his life for the sheep. . . . I am the good shepherd; I know my sheep and my sheep know me—just as the Father knows me and I know the Father—and I lay down my life for the sheep" (John 10:11, 14–15). God the Father overcame the fundamental problem of human sin by sending Jesus, his Son, into the world to live a sinless life and to become an acceptable sacrifice for the people he loved. "For God so loved the world that He gave His only begotten Son, that whoever believes in Him should not perish but have everlasting life" (3:16 NKJV). God sent a living copy of himself in the person of Jesus, born in a manger. Jesus used the metaphor of shepherd and sheep to teach his listeners what it means to be a good shepherd in contrast to a hired hand or a thief. Rather than take advantage of the sheep, the good shepherd protects them and is willing to die for them.

God is portrayed as the shepherd of his flock on many occasions in numerous Old Testament passages, and the people of Israel are referred to as the sheep of his pasture.[10] The use of shepherd and sheep in relationship to the people of Israel is a well-known metaphor for leaders, divine and human, such as Moses (Exodus 3:1), David (2 Samuel 5:2), and God (Psalm 23).[11] Jesus continued this line of thought during the Feast of Dedication in Jerusalem, in the temple area walking in Solomon's Colonnade. Jewish leaders challenged Jesus to admit whether he was the Messiah, the sent one of God. Jesus responded by saying, "My sheep listen to my voice; I know them, and they follow me. I give them eternal life, and they shall never perish; no one can snatch them out of my hand. My Father, who has given them to me, is greater than all; no one can snatch them out of my Father's hand. I and the Father are one" (John 10:27–30). Jesus clearly saw himself as related to God the Father, and in this case, he contended they were the same person.

Third Member of the Trinitarian Family

What about the third member of this family, the Holy Spirit? The Spirit of God was present at creation as the third agent in the beginning. The Genesis record says, "In the beginning God created the heavens and the earth. Now the earth was formless and empty, darkness was over the surface of the deep, and the Spirit of God was hovering over the waters" (Genesis 1:1–2). This passage is the prelude, setting the context for the creative work God did in the beginning.

King David was aware of the Spirit of God when he said, "Do not cast me from your presence or take your Holy Spirit from me," in his confession to God for his sins (Psalm 51:11). King David confessed the omnipresence of God's Spirit when he said,

> Where can I go from your Spirit? Where can I flee from your presence? If I go up to the heavens, you are there; if I make my bed in the depths, you are there. If I rise on the wings of the dawn, if I settle on the far side of the sea, even there your hand will guide me, your right hand will hold me fast. (Psalm 139:7–10)

King David was aware of the presence of the Spirit of God regardless of where he went.

The Holy Spirit was an active agent in the birth of Jesus. The Gospel of Matthew records Mary to be with child through the Holy Spirit (Matthew 1:18). God spoke to Joseph, the earthly father of Jesus, in a dream to explain how his betrothed wife, Mary, became pregnant. " 'The virgin will be with child and will give birth to a son, and they will call him Immanuel'—which means, 'God with us' " (1:23). The Holy Spirit of God was also present at the baptism of Jesus at the beginning of his ministry (3:16). Jesus was also led by the Spirit into the desert for a time of temptation (4:1). Jesus promised the coming of the Comforter, another name for the Holy Spirit, to his disciples as one who would come in his absence. The Holy Spirit's assignment was to teach and remind the disciples of Jesus of everything he taught them (John 14:25–27). Dr. Luke records the presence of the Holy Spirit in the first church, reminding them that "John baptized with water, but in a few days you will be baptized with the Holy Spirit" (Acts 1:5). The Holy Spirit was the presence of Jesus in spirit form to guide and empower the disciples (2:38).

The Holy Spirit is the third person of the plural God. We find God the Father, God the Son, and God the Spirit as the triune God, three persons in one, the Trinity. This is the Divine Family with interacting relationships, unique and complementary roles, acting in unity as one. The fundamental sense of community is found in God himself, in the Trinity. The trinitarian family is the essential notion and genesis for the human family. This is where the family began.

The Trinitarian Family

What are the implications of the trinitarian relationships for families today? The Trinity is a family of three persons: God the Father, God the Son, and God the Spirit. This truth, clearly demonstrated in scripture, is, on the one hand, extremely hard to grasp, yet on the other hand, it is so clear. It is simplicity in complexity. While the Trinity may not look like human families with a father, mother, and children, they nevertheless form a family in a divine way.

The three-person God of the Trinity relates to one another like three persons in a dance. George Cladis used the metaphor of a dance to describe the working relationship of the Trinity as a team in collaboration. He cites John of Damascus, a Greek theologian of the seventh century, and his use of the word *perichoresis* to describe the Trinity. Cladis reports that *perichoresis* means literally "circle dance." *Choris* in ancient Greek referred to a round dance performed at banquets and festive occasions. The verb form, *choreuo*, means to dance in a round dance, which included singing. The English word *chorus* is a derivation of this word. Cladis pointed to the prefix *peri*, meaning (in Greek) "round about" or "all around," emphasizing the circularity of the holy dance envisioned by John. Cladis contends that a perichoretic image of the Trinity is that of the three persons of God in constant movement in a circle that implies intimacy, equality, unity yet distinction, and love.[12] The description Cladis used from

John of Damascus is helpful as we think of human families and relationships. Cladis also cited theologian Shirley Guthrie, who refers to the Trinity doing choreography like a ballet. She refers to the circle dance of God with a sense of joy, freedom, song, intimacy, harmony, and unity in a community of persons.[13]

We understand intimacy, equality, unity with distinction, and love in human families in the same way. We also experience joy, freedom, song, intimacy, harmony, unity, and community in families. The Trinity, as revealed by God in scripture, points us to relationships in the Divine Family and helps us understand who we are and how we might relate in human families. Erickson supports the teaching of Tertullian, an early church father, who said, "The doctrine of the Trinity must be divinely revealed, not humanly constructed." We do not hold to this belief because it is self-evident or logically cogent. We hold it to be true because God has revealed that this is what he is like. Someone once said, "To try to explain it, you'll lose your mind. But try to deny it, and you'll lose your soul."[14]

Principles for Family Hope

The plan for community for human families comes from God's nature as a Triune God. This plan represents his own revelation to humanity and his plan for human families. There are several implications from the Divine Family for human families. Family members in a human family are connected relationally. DNA present in biological families connects us scientifically. Families by choice, through adoption or foster care, have chosen to be related. There is a sense of love, commitment, and unity in families also seen in the Trinity. Family members can experience love through extraordinarily strong ties, loyalty, and commitment. Ideally, each family member has a role to play as father, mother, son, or daughter. Ideally, family members work together for the benefit of one another and in many cases for a sense of mission as a family. There is a sense of belonging. A father and mother say, "This is our son" or "This is our daughter." There is a sense of family identity.

In the case of your family, you have a history, a past, a legacy, a particular DNA running through your blood, and a sense of life mission. You see your family members. You face one another. You share the dance of life—good, bad, right, wrong—together as a family. You belong to one another. You are devoted to one another. You protect one another. You sacrifice for one another. You work toward the good of each member of the family. You celebrate together. You mourn together. You live life together. You can hurt, harm, help, assist, offend, confess, forgive, serve, honor, cherish, and reconcile family relationships as modeled by God the Father, God the Son, and God the Holy Spirit. You are a family just like God in the Trinity is family. Viewing your family from a trinitarian perspective helps view your own families with a new and fresh perspective.

The Trinity, the Divine Family, provides a model for human families as its precedent. We know how to be good, healthy, and strong families from the example of God the Father, God the Son, and God the Spirit as recorded in scripture. How does this high ideal play out in the first human family?

Questions for Reflection

1. What is your reaction to the Divine Family? In what ways do you think of the Trinity as family?
2. How does the Trinity shape your understanding of families today?
3. What might we learn from the Divine Family that has a bearing on your family?
4. How are the relationships of the Divine Family similar or different from human families?
5. What qualities of the Divine Family do you desire for your family?

Chapter 3

THE FIRST FAMILY

Adam, Eve, Cain, and Abel

You don't choose your family. They are
God's gift to you, as you are to them.

—Desmond Tutu

Adam and Eve are the first couple in human history, according to the Judeo-Christian tradition of faith and the record of Holy Scripture. They are also the first couple who bore children: Cain and Abel. They are the first human family, the first parents. How would they reflect the Divine Family?

The First Family becomes a living image of God in relationships among one another. We have much to learn from how the family was formed. We can learn lessons from the birth and life of the first two children born to the First Family. We have much to learn from this First Family that may apply to our families today. We have much to learn from the source of truth and knowledge on these matters.

Dietrich Bonhoeffer wrote, "Humankind no longer lives in the beginning—it has lost the beginning. Now it finds itself in the middle, knowing neither the end nor the beginning, and yet knowing that it is in the middle and must move on toward the end. It sees that its life is determined by these two facets, of which it knows only that it does not know them."[1] Bonhoeffer suggests that since we have no experience of the beginning or the end, we have no outside observer on whom we can depend other than what is revealed to us in language and terms we can understand. He calls this the language of the middle. For us, it is the witness of the Bible in Genesis.

In Genesis 1, we learn that God created a man and a woman in his own image. God blessed them and gave them the assignment of being fruitful and increasing in number, of populating the earth, and of managing it as stewards in charge (Genesis 1:26–31). Beyond these initial instructions, Genesis 2 provides additional information about the conditions under which Adam and Eve would live in the garden of Eden, in the east. Eden included trees, a river with four headwaters, a garden, winds, gold, aromatic resin, and onyx. Adam and Eve were to manage the garden and were prohibited from eating from the Tree of Knowledge of Good and Evil, with a consequence of death if they broke that rule. The end of chapter 2 describes the creation of Eve as a suitable helper for Adam. God placed Adam into a deep sleep, then took a rib from his side and formed Eve. When Adam saw Eve he said, "This is now bone of my bones and flesh of my flesh; she shall be called 'woman,' for she was taken out of man" (2:23). The author of Genesis finished this chapter by saying "For this reason a man will leave his father and mother and be united to his wife, and they will become one flesh. The man and his wife were both naked, and they felt no shame" (2:24–25).

In Genesis 3, the story of the First Family and their graceful beginning takes a turn for the worse with disobedience to God's one rule: do not eat from the Tree of Knowledge of Good and Evil. The serpent tempted Eve by questioning God's instruction. She ate fruit from the tree and shared it with Adam. As a result, they were banished from the garden of Eden to work and toil the ground with hard labor and sweat and to procreate through painful birth.

Genesis 4 could be titled "Life Outside the Garden of Eden." This is the context for the story of the First Family.[2] Their story begins to unfold in a less than perfect environment. Sin has entered the story and begins a trend toward a departure from God's design for humanity, and the consequences that follow include rebellion. This chapter records the first children born to Adam and Eve. The First Family begins to multiply, to find their vocation, to engage in worship by presenting offerings to God from the fruit of their labor, and to experience the first homicide recorded in human history.

The First Family Multiplies

The biblical record says that Adam *knew* Eve. The Hebrew word translated "knew" is *yādā* which means a sexual relationship, to fully know each other where reproduction is involved.[3] Cohabitation is a means to an end—a deeper, more intimate knowledge of each other, and a unique relationship. Upon giving birth to Cain, Eve says, "I have acquired a man from Yahweh."[4] The word she used is *qānâ*, indicating Eve has created a man with help from the Lord. Eve's exclamation reflects her faith and dependence on the Lord and the veracity of God's word to her.[5] Adam had sexual intercourse with Eve again, and she gave birth to Abel, the second son.

Later in this story, Adam lay with Eve again, and she gave birth to another son, Seth (Genesis 4:25). Chapter 5 records Adam and Eve having additional sons and daughters (v. 4). Cain lay with his wife, and she gave birth to a son, Enoch (4:17). Enoch had sons, and the story of multiplication of humans continues in this way (4:18). Generations of humans have been born through the reproductive means of sexual intercourse, just like the children of the first couple in the First Family. God assigned specific tasks to Adam and Eve to care for creation and serve as stewards of the world, which would be required to sustain these growing families. This work would include the care and concern for the land, for animals, the cultivation of crops, production of food, and managers of all that God provided.

The First Family Works

Cain, the first son, is a tiller of the soil—a farmer, like his father, Adam. Cain found his work as a servant of the ground. Abel, on the other hand, finds work as a keeper of the flocks, a shepherd.[6] Abel was followed in his vocation by people like Jacob (Genesis 30:36), Joseph (37:2), Moses (Exodus 3:1), and David (1 Samuel 16:11; 17:34). Later in the story, Cain transitions from working as a farmer to a city builder.[7] Work was part of the life experience of the First Family. The act of work is a gift from God, an assigned task to be completed as part of the fulfillment of life purpose. The conditions of work are cursed due to the fall but not work itself. Work was embraced and expected of each son. It appears that each son was given the freedom to explore and embrace different ways of working and passion for work. Work is an honorable activity that produces a reward and results in a sense of satisfaction. Worship and thanksgiving for the fruits of their labor would naturally accompany work.

The First Family Worships

As the First Family grew and multiplied, family members began to express their vocational choices with yield from the land and from livestock. Patterns of worship and thanksgiving became part of family life. It is not surprising to enter a scene of worship as a logical next part of the story. The First Family demonstrated their acknowledgment of God as creator and sustainer of life for this family and sought to worship and give thanks to him. What is surprising is the way in which the worship experience ends. While there is no mention of an altar where worship sacrifices and offerings are made to God, the two brothers practice worship and thanksgiving by bringing offerings to the Lord as an act of worship.

Each brother brought a *minḥâ* appropriate to his occupation. A *minḥâ* could refer to any offering of grain, but animals might also be included as a tribute to secure goodwill. It could also consist of choice flour or grain, cereal, to which oil and frankincense could be added to form baked loaves, wafers, or morsels. Firstfruits would have been the first grains to ripen each season and were to be brought to the Lord as an offering.[8] Cain brought "some of the fruits of the soil as an offering," and Abel brought "fat portions from some of the first-born of his flock" (Genesis 4:3–4).

The Lord looked with favor on Abel's offering but did not respond in the same way with Cain. Cain reacted with anger "and his face was downcast" (v. 5). The text says Cain was "very angry." This type of anger is often a prelude to homicidal acts.[9] Some commentators suggest Cain made an error when selecting his offering. While Cain's offering was an expression of his vocation, he brought neither firstlings nor firstfruits.[10] The Law of the Lord was insistent that all firstlings must be offered in sacrifice or redeemed. The first-born by right belong to God, so every human firstborn had to be redeemed. In all animal sacrifices, the fat was burnt because it, too, belonged to the Lord, being regarded as the choicest part of the animal.[11] Most commentators agree that the quality of the offering was at the heart of the issue of rejection of Cain's gift.[12] The focus here is on the intention and attitude of the giver. It was the integrity of the gift that was at stake.[13] Cain's gift was more common, while Abel's gift was of the finest quality.[14] The first scene of this worship experience is disappointing and surprising. However, the conversation that follows is even more intriguing and unexpected.

God Provides a Way Out

God noticed Cain's anger and downcast face, yet it is challenging to pinpoint the focus of Cain's anger. Is he angry with God, with Abel, or with himself?[15] God asks Cain: "Why are you angry? Why is your face downcast?" (Genesis 4:6) One commentator asserts that a face downcast indicated depression rather than anger. Depression is anger turned inward. The Lord is attentive to Cain and noticed his facial expressions and body posture. This indicates a concern with how Cain was responding to the rejection of his gift. God began to offer "fatherly advice to Cain as a way out before it is too late."[16]

The text does not mention Adam or Eve in this conversation. While they may have been present, there is no indication they were engaged in this crucial conversation between Cain and God. We are not aware of the training and instruction Adam and Eve may have provided Cain as to the proper ways to present an offering to the Lord. It is God who engages Cain like a son. God takes on the role of father who engages Cain at this low point in his life. God is present and available as a heavenly father.

God not only engages but intervenes once Cain's response to correction is evident. He asked Cain, "If you do what is right, will you not be accepted?" (v. 7). The New American Standard Bible (1995) records this question as "If you do well, will not your countenance be lifted up?" Von Rad suggests this phrase could be translated as "If you do well, there is lifting up, you can freely lift up your face."[17] Hamilton, another commentator, suggests this understanding of the sentence: "He who now bows his head will be able to hold his head high."[18] Hamilton adds a contrast to right choices by adding, "Look, if you have behaved well you will be at ease. But if you have not, sin will be lurking at your door."[19]

Sin is now personified as an actor in the story. The text says, "Sin is crouching at your door, it desires to have you, but you must master it" (Genesis 4:7). The Akkadian word for *sin* here is *rābiṣu*, meaning various officials including demons, especially those that guard entrances to buildings.[20] Rabbi Ben Yashar suggests translating verse 7 as "Is it not this way? If you do well, there is the honour due to the first-born. If you do not do well, sin crouches for the first-born." Yashar suggests Cain, the first-born, has special responsibilities, especially in worship. If he carries them out, he will enjoy the privileges associated with his primacy.[21] God is saying demons are crouching at your doorstep ready to pounce on you if you do not master this moment. The central scene of this story hangs on this moment, this opportunity to reconsider, to gather one's thoughts, to regain one's composure. Cain's reaction to God's disapproval is paramount over the quality of his offering. What matters most at this point is the management of Cain's emotions, feelings, and thoughts. He can change his trajectory if he will.

Murder in the First Family

Cain appears to ignore the way out as well as the recommendations provided by God and moves out in his own way to resolve the emotions he felt at that time. Rather than mastering the croucher at the doorstep, Cain invites him in and submits to the temptation to resolve the conflict in a sinful manner. Sin masters Cain. Cain makes matters worse. Cain invites Abel out to the field. While they are in the field, Cain attacks his brother, Abel, and kills him (Genesis 4:8). Wenham suggests Cain's invitation to Abel to go out to the field was an effort to get out of range of help and is proof of premeditation. In Hebrew, the words for "attacked" are *wayyāqom qayin*, meaning ruthless violence by private persons. Cain was unable to restrain his resentment and bitterness, and kills the only scapegoat available: his brother, Abel.[22]

Honestly, my heart is broken as I write these words. How could an act of worship of the one true God end in the murder of a sibling? Where does the First Family go so wrong? This story is a shocking reminder that the heart of every human is vulnerable to sin. If not mastered, it has the power to lead us to do the most unimaginable deed, murder.

God Investigates Murder in the First Family

God continues to pursue the matter with Cain through interrogation, prosecution, punishment, promise-making, and redemption. God is concerned about the sins we commit against each other—in families and in society in general.[23] Even in our sin and rebellion, God, as a father, faithfully and relentlessly pursues us with grace and mercy. His first question to Cain is, "Where is your brother, Abel?" This question echoes the question God asked Adam when he took a bite of the fruit in the garden of Eden. God asked Adam, "Where are you?" God obviously knew where Adam was just as he knew where Abel was. God's question is rhetorical, designed to invite Cain to acknowledge his responsibility for his brother and draw attention to the fraternal relationship.[24]

Cain answers with a bald-faced lie. He says, "I don't know," and follows this lie with a question: "Am I my brother's keeper?" (v. 9). Cain's question could be understood as "Am I the shepherd's shepherd?"[25] The word for "guardian" is *šōmēr*, suggesting a legal term for a person entrusted with the custody and care of an object. In this verse, the use of *šōmēr* may imply legal responsibility to Cain for Abel. The phrase "to keep" means not only to preserve and sustain but to control, regulate, and exercise authority over. Cain's question appears to be evasive and indifferent to the responsibility for his brother, who is now dead.[26] Wenham notes that the biblical law required a brother to be the first to assist, yet Cain seems hardened to this idea.[27]

Prosecution and Punishment

God shifts from interrogation to prosecution. He asked Cain, "What have you done?" (Genesis 4:10). God hears Abel's blood crying from the ground. These four words shaped into a penetrating question represent a "whole theology whose principles inform much of the criminal and cultic law of Israel. Life is in the blood, so shed blood is the most polluting of all substances."[28] The word for crying is *sā aq*, frequently describing the cry of the oppressed, the overworked, and the exhausted Israelites in Egypt or the afflicted stranger, widow, or orphan as well as the groans of the innocent victim who is brutalized and harassed.[29] The word can also convey the cry of men without food, expecting to die, or the scream of a woman being raped, and the plea to God of victims of injustice.[30]

The spilling of blood is a serious matter. According to Old Testament tradition, blood and life belong to God alone. When a man commits murder, he attacks God's right of possession. As such, buried blood cries out to the Lord of life.[31] We must not lose track of this truth. The image of God, the *imago Dei*, is embedded into the life of every human and provides implications for interpersonal and social justice.[32] How we treat each other matters to God. Every person is made in God's image, is known by God, even the number of hairs on our head (Matthew 10:30), and is important to God and, by implication, should be of importance to us. The conversation moves from prosecution to punishment. Cain is guilty of murder and is indifferent toward his brother, Abel.

God changes the subject to punishment. God issues a curse on Cain's vocation providing no further yield from the ground through crops. Cain will become a restless wanderer on the earth with no home and no family—alone. The deepest impact of this punishment is the banishment of Cain from his family. All relationships with his family are broken. His relationship with God is also broken.[33] As a result of Cain's disobedience, God's judgment results in severe consequences. Cain loses all sense of belonging and identification with a community. He becomes rootless and detached.[34]

In fact, the sentence is so harsh that Cain objects with a grievance. Cain said, "My punishment is more than I can bear" (Genesis 4:13). Cain objects with four issues: There will only be meager results from his labor, he is now hidden from the face of God, he is destined to live as a nomad, and he is vulnerable to any assailant who may wish him harm. Ironically, the man who killed his brother now fears someone else will kill him.[35] It appears that alienation from God leads to fear of others.

Another irony is that this story began with an effort to draw near to God and ends with separation from God because of sin, pride, disobedience, and rebellion.[36] In Cain's rebellion and objection to his punishment, God is still listening, flexible, responsive. Even in judgment and punishment, God interjects grace and loving care. He added a promise of protection to Cain. God said, "Not so, if anyone kills Cain, he will suffer vengeance seven times over" (Genesis 4:15).

Cain does not have the final word in this matter; God does. He provides protection for Cain.[37] The Lord sealed the promise with a "mark" on Cain so no one who found him would kill him. While we do not know what kind of mark was placed on Cain, commentators suggest the mark could be a sign of God's power, a symbol of association, or a sign of cognition on the part of the observer.[38] Following this promise, Cain left Eden toward the land of Nod, east of Eden, to begin the rest of his life. But the story does not end there.

God Redeems the First Family

What has gone terribly wrong is not beyond the redemptive hand of God in human history. Cain is banned because he broke God's rule. He is destined to live a life of alienation but not without purpose. Although he is banned, God chooses to also bless him.[39] In his new life, east of Eden and west of Nod, Cain finds a wife, lays with her, and has children. A common and often unresolved question in this story is where Cain, the firstborn of the first couple, might have found a wife. Jim Denison wrestled with this question and suggested it is quite possible Cain married his sister.[40] However, these possibilities generate more questions about incest. One author suggests that genetic mutations were not common concerns in the beginning and not prohibited until the Mosaic law was developed two thousand five hundred years later, clearly stating marriage between relatives was not permitted.[41]

Cain's new mission in life was to become a city builder. Enoch, his firstborn, found a wife and had Irad, who had Mehujael, who had Methushael, who had Lamech. Lamech had three sons: Jabal lived in tents and worked with livestock; Jubal was a musician who played various instruments; and Tubal-Cain was a blacksmith who worked with bronze and iron. Adam and Eve had a third son, Seth, as they reflected on the loss of Abel, and Seth fathered Enosh during a time in which men began to call on the name of the Lord (Genesis 4:17–26). Some commentators suggest that Cain's city building was an early prototype of the cities of refuge since murder was punishable by death.[42] Sailhamer suggests that the final part of Cain's story and his descendants constitutes the theme of forgiveness and redemption.[43] What was intended for harm became a vehicle for good and for limiting violence and harm in the world through the family and descendants of Cain.

Principles for Family Hope

The story of the First Family generates several key principles to live by and to apply to modern-day families. These principles might be applied personally in our relationship to God. The principles are also applicable to our interpersonal relationships between us and others. Here are a few to consider:

Work Is Good. Cain's work as a farmer and Abel's work as a shepherd were equally honorable. All work is a gift from God, which means all work is honorable and good. Another word for *work* is *vocation*, from the Latin word *vocare*, which means "to call." Some people refer to their work as a calling. There is a sense in which God calls us to a personal relationship with him that includes confession of sin, an admission that we need a savior, and a faith commitment of trust in his provision of grace for us through the life of his Son, Jesus Christ. This faith relationship redeems all God intended for each of us and can be expressed in the work we are called to do.

I am not limiting this call to a call to vocational ministry reserved for ministers and pastors but a life vocation connected to God's redemptive purpose in human history. This is how the apostle Paul expressed a call to work: "For it is by grace you have been saved, through faith—and this is not from yourselves, it is the gift of God— not by works, so that no one can boast. For we are God's handiwork, created in Christ Jesus to do good works, which God prepared in advance for us to do" (Ephesians 2:8–10 NIV). God planned the work we are called to do in advance. Work is a blessing when we realize our work connects to God's redemptive work in human history. This means our work matters to God. When we work with this perspective, we look for and find God in our work, which enables us to be encouraged and enthused in his presence—even on bad days.

God Engages Us Daily. Even today, God continues to engage us and intervene when we respond to his instruction, laws, and commandments in negative and rebellious ways. In the same way God engaged Cain, he speaks to us through his Spirit to prompt, remind, and nudge us toward better responses, better behavior, and a better way. He is a good, good father who pursues us when we go astray.

God Provides a Way Out. There was a way out if Cain had paused, counted to ten, reconsidered, reflected, and allowed the counsel and wisdom of God to sink in. How many times does God engage us in a conversation at these key moments, at the precipice of family conflict and disaster? On a flight, I met a fellow passenger. I told him about my work. He seemed to listen carefully and intently to my story. After the flight, he handed me a slip of paper. I put it in my pocket to read later. When I arrived at the hotel, I began to get comfortable and prepare for the next day's business. I pulled the slip of paper the young man gave me from my shirt pocket and read these words: "1 Peter 5:8." This verse says: "Be self-controlled and alert. Your enemy the devil prowls around like a roaring lion looking for someone to devour." I never saw this young man again, nor can I remember his face, but I have never forgotten his note to me. I felt as if he was trying to warn me even though we were strangers. I took his message to heart, and I recognized him as a messenger from God.

God Encourages Mastery over Our Emotions. Satan and his demons are focused on destroying what was meant for good, even in worship. Pride, envy, jealousy, anger, and rage are all poisons that invade our family relationships and can end in disaster if not mastered. These human emotions and actions tear at the fabric of community in the most intimate of relationships. The apostle Paul wrote these words to Christians at the church in Ephesus encouraging them to put off these actions, like removing outer garments and replacing them with garments of the new life in Christ: "Get rid of all bitterness, rage and anger, brawling and slander, along with every form of malice. Be kind and compassionate to one another, forgiving each other, just as in Christ God forgave you" (Ephesians 4:31–32). The decision to get rid of these emotions and actions resulting in sin is an act of the will. It is a choice we must make on a daily, and sometimes moment by moment, basis. To fail to make the right decisions at these inflection points could lead down a slippery slope of sin and unthinkable consequences. Even in our sin, God continues to pursue us.

We Are Responsible for One Another. This is the fiber of relationships in community. I can't recall when I understood I was responsible for my two brothers, and they became responsible for me. This is something our parents constantly communicated, taught, and expected of us. The question "Where is your brother?" echoes in my mind even though my brothers and I are in our fifties and sixties with our own families and living in different cities. I call them regularly, sometimes weekly and at least monthly. I call my mother, a widow now, weekly, sometimes more than once a week. We stay in touch. I cannot imagine any other way to live. I check on my brothers-in-law and my mother-in-law, too, but not quite as often. Why? Because I feel responsible. I am responsible. They are my family. I cannot fathom siblings who have not spoken with each other for months or years. This does not compute to my understanding of what being family means.

We named our youngest son Thomas Rafael Reyes after a ministry colleague who has impacted most of my adult life and ministry, Dr. Thom Wolf. We affectionately refer to him as Brother Thom or Dr. Thom. Over the years, we have had occasions to connect our Tommy with Brother Thom in our home. Brother Thom took our choice of naming Tommy after him very seriously. When Tommy was about three years old, he asked my wife, Belinda, an intriguing question after Brother Thom left our home in San Antonio after a brief visit. He asked, "Mommy, does Brother Thom belong to me?" She said, "Yes, he belongs to you, and you belong to him." This seemed to satisfy his inquiring mind.

The truth is that we are in relationships with one another in community, and we belong to one another. We are responsible to and for one another. This is the essence of family and familial relationships. This may be a clue as to the significance of the ongoing conversation between God and Cain about Abel's murder. God continued the conversation with Cain to drive home the gravity of his actions and to impress upon Cain his responsibility for his brother.

God's Grace Abounds. At the point of this tragic murder in the First Family, I could not imagine a single good outcome. One commentator asserts that the end of this story constitutes God's forgiveness for Cain, yet not without consequences. Grace appears in the earliest place in the Old Testament text rather than being delayed or assigned to the New Testament alone.[44] The first human family is crushed by the same thing that ejected them from the garden of Eden—sin. Sin, our choice to rebel against the character of God, the Law of God, the rules for living he has given us, creates consequences of the worst magnitude, even murder. Sin, disobedience, and rebellion cannot be underestimated as they relate to healthy and effective families. It threatens the core of our existence. It poisons and kills our relationships. It is a crouching lion poised at the doorstep of every family, ready to pounce, to kill, to steal, and to destroy all that God has intended for good. Yet the gift of God's grace helps redeem families even when terrible things happen. God's grace provides forgiveness, restoration, reconciliation, and a way forward in family relationships even when consequences are permanent. God's gift of a family is intended for blessing, not a curse. God's plan is for us to live in harmony in families.

Families Are for Community. Families are created for community and relationships, forever. How we relate to one another matters. How we treat one another matters. How we view one another matters. How we understand one another and live out a sense of belonging and responsibility for the well-being of each person matters. This is God's design for families. But even when we fall short and sabotage our own existence as a family, the redemptive arm of God is not so short that he cannot reach into our mess and bring a message of hope and redemption. The prophet Isaiah said, "Surely the arm of the Lord is not too short to save, nor his ear too dull to hear" (Isaiah 59:1).

Summary

If your family is undergoing a struggle, a problem, a major conflict, appeal to the Lord and place the matter in his hands. Pray for wisdom, for help, for resolution. Pray for a miracle to invade your family. Pray for "strength for today and bright hope for tomorrow."[45] Know this: his arm is not too short that he cannot reach you and intervene. His ear is more attentive to your heart's cry than you may realize. He is listening, and he will respond. He never sleeps. He is always watching over his own, as a good father should. You did not choose your family. God did. He chose your family for a reason and a purpose. Trust him to take what was intended for harm and pray for his turning it toward good—for you, for others, for his name, for his will, and for his kingdom. My encouragement to you and your family is based on the promises of God. He always keeps his promises. Let's explore how he keeps his promises with the Promised Family.

Questions for Reflection

1. In what ways are you surprised that the first murder in human history started out as a worship service?

2. How is worship connected to family relationships?

3. How do we know Cain had a way out to avoid murdering his brother Abel?

4. How is God's grace seen in the life of Cain?

5. How do we know God can carry out his purpose through us even when we sin?

Chapter 4

THE PROMISED FAMILY

Abraham, the First Generation of Promise

Let us hold unswervingly to the hope we profess,
for he who promised is faithful.

—Hebrews 10:23

Have you ever made a promise and then did everything you could to keep it? Promises seem sacred, like a vow. It is the act of giving your word that you will do something and then getting it done. God makes promises, too, and keeps them. He made many promises to a man named Abram and to his family.

The Promised Family begins with the calling of Abram in Genesis 12. Some say Genesis 12 could be the first chapter in the Bible with the previous eleven chapters as an introduction.[1] Prior to the calling of Abram, the Genesis writer chronicles the story of Noah and his sons: Shem, Ham, and Japheth in Genesis 5 and the flood in Genesis 6 through 9. In Genesis 10, a listing of the table of nations from the families of Shem, Ham, and Japheth appears. In Genesis 11, the story of the Tower of Babel unfolds, where inhabitants of the earth shared one language in the plain of Shinar in modern-day Iraq. The vision of the people who settled there is recorded as "Come, let us build ourselves a city, with a tower that reaches to the heavens, so that we may make a name for ourselves and not be scattered over the face of the whole earth" (Genesis 11:4). God had other plans to confuse their language and scatter people all over the face of the earth. The story of the Promised Family and call of Abram is a gift to the people of the earth amid strong judgment of humankind at Babel.[2] Among the people scattered throughout the earth was Terah, the father of Abram. Terah took his son Abram, Abram's wife, Sarai, and his grandson Lot, son of Haran, and set out from Ur of the Chaldeans to go to Canaan but settled short of there in Haran.

An Avalanche of Blessing

The calling of Abram is one of the most significant migration events in human history.[3] It is through this human migration that God's unfolding purpose and plan for his people emerges. A land was needed for a nation of people who would do righteousness and justice.[4] God promised to birth a nation from one man and introduced his plan of redemption for the entire world through Abram.[5] The call of Abram includes the promise of a blessing if Abram obeys. One commentator refers to the promise as "an avalanche of blessings," which included land, a nation from Abram's seed, and unimaginable resources. The way of life and blessing once marked by the Tree of Knowledge of Good and Evil, then by Noah's ark, is now marked by the identification with Abram and his seed.[6] The blessing promises a plan for redemption for the scattered nations and extends to the whole world.[7]

At this time in human history, social organization of people existed in the form of tribes, which were the largest units of social organization. A tribe consisted of clans where kinship and geography served as identifying a group of people. The clan played an intermediate role between the tribe and the nuclear family.

The family was the father's household, the smallest unit and most important to an individual. The father was the head over wives and unmarried daughters, and he governed individual behavior with implications for the whole family. God called Abram to cut ties with the most important social unit in his life, his family. The command required Abram leave his home in Northern Mesopotamia.[8] The call of Abram started with a command backed by several promises from God that outweighed the requirement of obedience.[9] Abram's response was obedience to God's command to leave his home country and go to a place God would show him. While a command would be reason enough to comply, the promises God outlined for Abram provided numerous motivations to follow God's instructions to move to a land unknown at this point.

The Promise of Land. The first promise is a promise of land. God said to Abram, "Leave your country, your people and your father's household and go to the land I will show you" (Genesis 12:1). The only road map Abram had was this command to obey. No land was specified, no direction was specified, and all Abram had was a word from the Lord in the form of a command to be obeyed.[10] Abram is called to leave the past and trust God with the future. To leave is an act of loyalty and a willingness to act and obey a command with the promise of a land in the future.

The Promise of a Nation. The second promise is a promise of a new people. God said to Abram, "I will make you into a great nation and I will bless you" (Genesis 12:2). God's promise depends on the opening or closing of the womb of Abram's wife, Sarai. What seems impossible to Abram is possible with God. The promise implies a vigorous and distinguished people. The shift to a "great" nation implies a land, nationhood, status, stability, government, and territory where this promise will manifest itself.[11] This promise includes a people that will be blessed with wealth, robust livestock, precious metals, gold, silver, human labor, slaves, and foreigners.[12] The blessing in human terms also means well-being, long life, peace, good harvest, and children.[13] The blessing will carry with it material increase, physical fruitfulness, and innumerable descendants.[14] God will deliver on this promise as the second installment of the avalanche of blessing. God alone is the source of all good fortune. What modern secular people refer to as good luck, the Old Testament witness refers to as blessing.[15]

The Promise of a Great Name. God promises Abram, "I will make your name great" (v. 2). This promise stands in contrast to the vision of the people gathered at Shinar to build the Tower of Babel and make a great name for themselves. The power to do this rests in the hands of God, not in human effort. Across the generations, the influence of Abram has impacted Judaism, Christianity, and Islam as world religions.[16] There is a purpose and a mission in being blessed in the next promise.

The Promise to Be a Blessing. God said to Abram, "and you will be a blessing" (Genesis 12:2). Abram will become the embodiment of blessing from God. He will be the source of all blessing to human families.[17] The Lord is the dispenser of the blessing,[18] and Abram became a receptacle and a transmitter of God's blessing.[19] The blessing is unchangeable and is capable of blessing and curse. The impact of the blessing through Abram is not limited to Abram's own good but extends to other people as well, even those beyond Abram's family and descendants.

The Promise of Blessing and Curse. God said to Abram, "I will bless those who bless you, and whoever curses you I will curse" (v. 3). This promise is like two sides of the same coin. The overarching purpose of God is to bless Abram and bless others through him. The threat of a curse thwarts any effort to undo God's intention to bless the nations and families of the earth.

The Promise to Bless the Nations. God said to Abram, "And all peoples on earth will be blessed through you" (v. 3). The avalanche of blessing has the entire earth and all its people from every tribe, language, and nation as its target. The grand finale of the avalanche of blessing is that all the earth's clans, peoples, and families will be blessed through Abram.[20] This promise is echoed by the apostles Peter and Paul in the New Testament.[21] The final portion of the promised blessing to Abram expresses God's plan for redemption for all of humanity.

Backing the Promises

Abram did as the Lord commanded, and Lot went with him. Abram and his wife, Sarai, set out with all their belongings to Canaan. He stopped at Shechem and built an altar to the Lord there. He did the same at Bethel and then set out for the Negev desert. Since there was a famine in the Negev, Abram traveled to Egypt. The pharaoh of Egypt expressed interest in Sarai. Abram told Sarai to say he was her brother for fear for his life. Pharaoh took Sarai into his palace because of her striking beauty. He then became inflicted with an illness and learned Sarai was really Abram's wife. Pharaoh summoned Abram to confront him and sent him away with sheep, cattle, donkeys, servants, and camels (Genesis 12:4–20). Abram and Lot separated from each other. Lot decided to move near Sodom and Gomorrah while Abram settled in the land of Canaan. Lot became a captive of kings in conflict in Sodom and Gomorrah and was rescued by Abram. Following these events, Abram began to wonder about God's promises.

Even with the overwhelming avalanche of promises from God, Abram faced the reality of his advancing age and his barren wife. Abram, who is childless at this point, wonders if God intends the blessings to come through Abram's servant Eliezer. All the tents that surrounded Abram's tent resonated with the shouts and noises of the children of other men in his camp.[22] The voices of children formed a backdrop to promises of a child to come. To die childless and leave no namesake on the earth is a fate of extreme sadness. Therefore, the assurance of God's presence, in view of Abram's childlessness, brought very little hope and joy.[23]

God responds to Abram's concerns by sending "the word of the Lord . . . to Abram in a vision" (15:1). This phrasing indicates a prophetic revelation.[24] A vision like this would normally come at night.[25] The Lord said to Abram, "Do not be afraid, Abram. I am your shield, your very great reward" (Genesis 15:1). The encouragement to not be afraid indicates a message of salvation and is meant to encourage and provide comfort to a man who is childless.[26] God will save and provide a son. The idea that God is a shield is a military metaphor. God is a shield for faithful people.[27] Abram will have God's protection in all things.[28] Abram is reminded by God that he is his benefactor and will make good on his promises.[29]

Abram's response ushers in the first time Abram speaks to God in his calling experience. In previous engagements with God, Abram merely listens and obeys. Now he speaks and raises questions: What can you give me from these promises without a child? Will Eliezer, my servant, be the one who inherits my estate? Abram addresses the central issue of Genesis 15: the delay of God to deliver on his promises. There is a delay and a requirement to wait in hope.[30] The Lord's answer is swift and direct. He answers Abram and says Eliezer will not be his heir and that a son from his own body will be his heir.

God then invited Abram to come outside his tent to see a word picture in the sky. He said, "Look up at the heavens and count the stars—if indeed you can count them" (v. 5). The word translated "look" means a "long look." It will take a long look to grasp and count the number of stars in the sky. Even so, it will be impossible to number them.[31] Then he said to Abram, "So shall your offspring be" (v. 5). God's response to Abram implies a waiting period. Abram will have to wait on a divine promise that is already and not yet in reality. In other words, the divine promise of God ensures the promise will come to pass and, in that sense, already exists even though it has not come to pass chronologically. One commentator said, "Faith [is] waiting on God to 'make good' on his promises." In view of the impossibility of a pregnancy from an aging wife, God informs Abram that it will happen.[32] Abram will not only be the father of a son but also the father of a multitude of offspring—so many he will not be able to count them.[33] Abram must trust God to deliver on his promise rather than do what he can to obtain God's promise.

This is a trustful acceptance of a divine promise as an act of faith.[34] One commentator said, "It is in crisis situations that faith or the lack of it is revealed."[35] Abram responded with additional questions and a request for more proof. The Lord made a covenant with Abram and promised him and his descendants the land between the Nile River and the Euphrates River inhabited by ten tribes of people.

Waiting on the Promises

In Genesis 16, we find that ten years proved too long for Sarai to wait on God's promise. She decided to bring her own resources and take action to help God keep his promise to Abram.[36] Sarai owned an Egyptian slave named Hagar, whose name means "flee" in Arabic.[37] Hagar was presumably a gift from Pharaoh to Sarai when she was in his palace. Since she was a gift from Pharaoh, Hagar would have been of superior beauty and capacity to serve as a talented person.[38] Sarai's action is focused on persuading Abram to take Hagar into his tent for sexual relations to produce an heir since she had no more hope of being a mother at her age.[39] Sarai faces the reality that for the past ten years she has had nonfunctioning reproductive organs.[40] One commentator suggested Sarai's action was on par with Eve's intent to be like God—an attempt to circumvent God's plan of blessing in favor of ensuring a blessing of her own. Unfortunately, Sarai's plan did not meet with God's approval.[41]

Even so, Sarai's action was commonplace in her day. There was no greater sorrow for an Israelite or Oriental woman than childlessness. Von Rad reports that widespread legal customs at that time included a wife bringing to the marriage her own personal maid, who was not available to her husband as a concubine in the same way his own female slaves were. If she gave her personal maid to her husband, in the event of her own childlessness, the child born of the maid was considered the wife's child. The slave was born "on the knees of the wife," so that the child was symbolically from the womb of the wife herself. Von Rad concludes that from a legal and moral perspective, Sarai's proposal was completely according to custom.[42] In fact, according to old Assyrian marriage contracts, if within two years of marriage a wife has not produced an offspring for the husband, only she may buy a maidservant and, even later, after she procures somehow an infant for him, she may sell her maidservant whenever she pleases.[43]

One rabbinic explanation for Sarai's actions was that barrenness after a ten-year period was grounds for divorce in Ancient Near Eastern custom.[44] In the same way Abram gave Sarai to Pharaoh, now Sarai gives Hagar to Abram. Abram, the donor, becomes Abram, the receiver, and Sarai, the pawn, becomes Sarai, the initiator. Hagar has no choice in the matter. She is taken, then given. She becomes an instrument in this family narrative.[45] Even if this practice was normative in Sarai's day, was it prudent? Did God really need her help to deliver on his promise to Abram? Or did Sarai choose not to trust and believe God and take him at his word? Did her timetable for God's promises expire causing her to jump into action?

Schemes Instead of Promises

Sarai developed a scheme to head off the divine promise with a human solution by giving Hagar to Abram to produce an heir.[46] While Sarai is old and barren, Hagar is young and fertile, and she conceived a son. Sarai's scheme gives birth to unintended consequences. The first issue is that Hagar despises Sarai.[47] To despise someone was to consider someone lightly. Sarai's status was lowered in Hagar's esteem.[48] Sarai naturally sensed this disposition in her maidservant, became incredibly angry with the results of her own scheme,[49] and blamed Abram for the situation. Sarai appealed to the Lord to settle the matter. Sarai said to Abram, "You are responsible for the wrong I am suffering. I put my servant in your arms, and now that she knows she is pregnant, she despises me. May the Lord judge between you and me" (Genesis 16:5). There is no indication in the biblical record that Abram had any interest in Hagar.[50] Abram responded by sending Hagar back to her mistress and said, "Your maid is in your power; do to her what is good in your sight" (v. 6 NASB95).

Sarai's emotions took over and resulted in harsh treatment of Hagar. The text indicates Sarai exacted severe and humiliating punishment of Hagar to the point that Hagar chose to run away.[51] Dods suggests Sarai failed to recognize that Hagar was a woman with hopes and feelings, a life of her own. As such, Sarai chose to commit a wrong against her.[52]

This shift in the story places procreation rather than companionship as the core purpose of marriage, resulting in negative consequences.[53] The second consequence of this scheme is that a runaway slave carried Abram's only conceived and perceived heir-child into the desert, a justified action on Hagar's part given the harsh treatment she experienced.[54] Sarai took advantage of her power over Hagar, a foreign woman, and complicates her problem of barrenness.[55] The final and most long-lasting consequence is that Ishmael, Hagar's son, became a rival and threat to Sarai and Isaac, the promised son.[56] Dods asserts that "little did [Sarai] think when she persuaded Abram to take Hagar that she was originating a rivalry which has run with keenest animosity through all ages and which oceans of blood have not quenched." It becomes clear that from one man came two world religions: Christianity and Islam, its rival.[57] Like cascading water, one problem's apparent solution begins another problem and in turn another.[58] The price of choosing not to wait on God, not to believe his promises, and inserting one's own actions into God's plans brought devastating consequences. Yet, there is hope even in the most challenging of life's circumstances and in some of the most unexpected places.

Hope in the Desert

Hagar ran away toward the only place she knew as home: Egypt. She made her way through the desert toward the Egyptian border[59] and stopped at a well-known oasis between Kadesh and Bered, to reflect on her situation.[60] The well is located near Kadesh-Barnea, located in the Desert of Zin southwest of the Dead Sea. Pieters offers questions Hagar may have considered at the well: "Where do I go from here? Who would want a runaway slave? Who would care for a pregnant runaway slave?"[61] At this well, the angel of the Lord appears to Hagar and asks, "Where have you come from, and where are you going?" (Genesis 16:8). Hagar answers truthfully saying, "I'm running away from my mistress Sarai" (v. 8). The angel of the Lord gave Hagar specific instructions: "Go back to your mistress and submit to her. . . . I will so increase your descendants that they will be too numerous to count" (vv. 9–10). The angel also said, "You are now with child and you will have a son. You shall name him Ishmael, for the Lord has heard of your misery. He will be a wild donkey of a man; his hand will be against everyone and everyone's hand against him, and he will live in hostility toward all his brothers" (vv. 11–12).

Hagar obeyed the angel and named her son Ishmael, which means "God has heard."[62] She also provided a name for God who met her there at the well and spoke through an angel. She named God "You are the God who sees me," and named the well "Beer Lahai Roi," the well of the God who sees me. Hagar confessed, "I have now seen the One who sees me" (vv. 13–14).

This encounter sounds like it may have been a shocking experience. However, Pieters suggests Hagar, living in the camp of Abram, most likely heard Abram speak of God and faith in him.[63] The angel of the Lord provided a timely word to a very proud person and encouraged her to do the right thing.[64] The runaway Hagar showed evidence of an encounter with God through repentance and her agreement to obey and return to Sarai to submit to her.[65] Even at the edge of the desert, a pregnant runaway slave, alienated from the only family she knew, found hope and purpose for her life and, most importantly, a relationship with God. Abram was eighty-six years of age when Ishmael was born. How will the story of this family continue to unfold as Ishmael grows up in this unique family environment?

Chosen for a Covenant

Thirteen years later, when Ishmael was a teenager, God appeared to Abram again and spoke to him. For the past thirteen years, Abram had no word, no direct communication, and no message of any kind from God. He was left in a state of suspense and uncertainty about the future.[66] This time God commanded Abram to "walk before me and be blameless." God spoke to Abram and confirmed his covenant to expand Abram's family. He said, "I will . . . greatly increase your numbers" (Genesis 17:1–2). God's engagement of Abram this time included a worship encounter, a confirmed covenant, a name change for Abram, and a further unfolding of a promised family. The name God used for himself in this exchange with Abram was El Shaddai. The Septuagint translates the meaning of this name as "God Almighty"; however, more recent translations suggest this name could also mean "God all-knowing."[67] Perhaps Abram needed to know that God knows everything there is to know about his circumstances.

At the sound of God's voice, the promise of a covenant, and requirements of obedience, Abram fell face down, the kind of demeanor demonstrated to a superior.[68] God established his covenant with Abram. Until now, the word *covenant* meant that God was making a unilateral promise without any requirement from the receiver. Here, for the first time, God makes requirements of Abram for the covenant to be fulfilled, marking a true partnership between God and man.[69] The covenant included numerous descendants, a permanent relationship of Abram's descendants to God as God's own people, and all the land of Canaan for an everlasting possession.[70] Abram's part of the covenant includes the act of "walking before me" and "being blameless." Abram is to follow the command of God in complete obedience as the right response to God's covenant to include Sabbath observance, abstinence from eating blood, and circumcision.[71] This is a special moment that becomes a memorial of God's covenant with Abram.

To commemorate the covenant, God changed Abram's name to Abraham. *Abraham* means "the father of many nations," indicating the blessing of God will be channeled through Abraham to all humankind.[72] This marks the first time in the Scriptures that a person's name is changed.[73] But even more significant is the emphasis on Abraham as a chosen instrument for God's purpose. On three occasions, God uses the pronominal suffix *ka* for *you* in the covenant promise directed toward Abraham. God says, "I will cause you . . . make of you nations . . . from you." Abraham is clearly the man God has chosen for this covenant.[74] Sarai, in her old age, was to be the one through whom it would be demonstrated that God alone could fulfill his covenant promise.[75] Sarai's name was also changed. God instructed Abraham to no longer refer to his wife as Sarai but from now on she would be named Sarah, the mother of nations. Kings of peoples would come from her womb (Genesis 17:15–16). God initiated the covenant with Abraham, maintains it, and will bring it to fulfillment.

On three occasions (vv. 7, 13, 19), God says the covenant has an eternal timeline.[76] Even so, Abraham, after hearing Sarah would bear him a son at age ninety and name him Isaac (vv. 19–22) still struggled to believe what he was hearing. He fell face down again, laughed, and said to himself, "Will a son be born to a man a hundred years old? Will Sarah bear a child at the age of ninety?" (v. 17). His thoughts went toward Ishmael, the son he already had. Abraham asked God, in that incredible moment, to allow Ishmael to live under God's blessing. God agreed but quickly turned Abraham's attention to the promised son, Isaac.

The naming of Isaac is yet another commemoration of God's covenant with Abraham. Dods noted that both incredulity and laughter are mixed in this story. "It is they who expect things so incongruous and so impossible to nature unaided that they smile even while they believe, who will one day find their hopes fulfilled and their hearts running over with joyful laughter." Dods concluded that if our hearts are fixed only on what can be accomplished on our own, no great joy can ever be ours. However, if we frame our hope in accordance with the promise of God, one day we will be able to say, "God hath made me to laugh."[77] Faith becomes the firm persuasion that these things are so, and such enthusiasm provides a measure of independence and may be seen by an unbelieving world as insanity.[78] Abraham and Sarah found great joy in their future even at their age.

Transition to Beersheba, Land of the Philistines

The next scene of the Promised Family, in Genesis 18 includes a visitation of three men at Abraham's camp near Mamre. The Lord spoke to Abraham with Sarah listening and said Sarah would bear a son in one year. Sarah laughed and wondered how this would be possible. The Lord raised this question: "Is anything too hard for the Lord?" (Genesis 18:14).

After God's promise to bear a son to Abraham through Sarah, Abraham became aware of the Lord's plans to destroy Sodom and Gomorrah. Abraham pleaded with the Lord to spare the cities if he could find ten righteous people. Sadly, Abraham was not able to come up with ten citizens who were living righteous lives. Both Sodom and Gomorrah and all their citizens were destroyed by fire due to their wicked living.

In Genesis 20, Abraham moved to the region of Negev between Kadesh and the land of Shur. Abraham again represented Sarah as his sister rather than his wife for fear of death by King Abimelech, a collector of beautiful women. Abimelech summoned Sarah into his living space. The Lord appeared to him in a dream, warning him that Sarah was Abraham's wife. The next morning, Abraham was summoned and confronted by Abimelech who sent Abraham and Sarah on their way with sheep, slaves, and shekels for fear of God's wrath on them.

In Genesis 21, Isaac is born of Sarah in her old age as God has promised. Hagar, Sarah's maidservant, and Ishmael are sent away from Abraham's tent.

Principles for Family Hope

There are numerous principles for modern-day families to apply from the experience of the Promised Family. The Promised Family started with the call of Abram to leave his home, to follow God, and to obey him without question as a new nation was built. Principles from the lives of Abram, Sarai, Hagar, and Ishmael are foundational truths families can use today to find hope.

God of the Impossible. You may be facing impossible situations in your family. What seems impossible or unredeemable to you now is quite possible for God. What God has said, he will do. What he has promised, he will fulfill. God will never let us be content with anything short of what perfectly fulfills his perfect love and purpose.[79] What God requires of us is obedience and faithfulness. Jesus once said to a rich young ruler who struggled with personal wealth, "What is impossible with men is possible with God" (Luke 18:27). If you are facing an impossible situation in your family, just remember, the God of the impossible will fulfill his promises to us and act according to his redemptive purpose.

Faith and Provision. Life with God requires obedience and faith. Our faith in him requires our willingness to trust him, even with our children. We don't worship our children; we worship God. It is only when we lose our lives in God's purpose that we have a life worth living and a something worth dying for. In our darkest moments and in the submission of our will to him, he provides. This is what life in him is all about. Provision comes on the mountain of sacrifice for a family of faith, a family of promise.

Conflict in the Family of Faith. Conflict is inevitable in families. It is part of human nature. The question is not what we will do if we have conflict but how we will manage conflict when it arises. Families are wise to major in conflict management that involves offense, repentance, forgiveness, and reconciliation as well-worn habits practiced and taught to our children.

The Elder Serves the Younger. While this is a pattern in the Old Testament stories dating back to Cain and Abel, it is not prescriptive. Rather, the focus of this story is not the pattern established but the fact that human customs, cultures, and norms do not govern the will and purpose of God in families. God is sovereign and will engage as he pleases through, and sometimes despite, our customs and cultural norms. This truth points to God's grace and mercy too. He will grant us what we do not deserve and withhold the punishment we do deserve.

Sibling Rivalry in the Promised Family. An entire book could be written on this topic. Suffice it to say here that sibling rivalry should be anticipated, mitigated, and reshaped for siblings to bless one another. Train your children early to reconcile, restore relationships, and celebrate the victories of their siblings and comfort them in misfortune. Even sibling rivalry does not mute or thwart the grace, mercy, and promise of God.

Families Standing on the Promises. What God has promised, he will do. Human interference in the implementation of God's promise usually ends in tragedy, profound consequences, hurt, pain, confusion, and unnecessary heartache. Manipulation seldom ends well. God is not mocked. Let God be God. Our role is to be servants of his will and purpose. God does not now or ever need your help to carry out what he has promised. He wants us to be the people he created and inspires us to do good works. Our role is to trust and obey.

Favoritism in the Promised Family. There is no place for favoritism in families. The personality of one child might blend better with the character of one of the parents. Children and parents can sometimes reflect the notion that "opposites attract." Yet every effort should be made to understand, appreciate, and affirm differences as humans created in the image of God. Differences should be celebrated as unique creations of a sovereign God.

Messy Families and God's Promise. The plain truth is that the families in these stories are messy. They are human. They are sinful, imperfect. They are real. They are probably as messy as your family and mine. But that is OK because we are human, sinful, and messy. Thank God for his grace, mercy, redemption, and availability to us to find life in his purpose and his presence to help us learn how to live by faith and in a way that pleases him. Life is not about our families. Life is about a God who loves us and wants to accomplish his purpose through our families, as messy as they are. Our families represent the perfect laboratory to reveal his love for us.

Families Come in Different Shapes and Sizes. In the story of Abraham, Isaac, Jacob, and Esau, we find a childless couple in Abraham and Sarah. Childless couples abound today and form the basic family unit. Hagar became a single mother when she gave birth to Ishmael. She is destined to raise her son with no husband, with no family support, and in a strange land. She has no place to belong and form her family. Yet Hagar and her son form a basic family unit.

The story of Isaac and Rebekah ends with two sons who are estranged, away from home. Their nest becomes empty perhaps before it should have. Jacob and Esau are separated as enemies and raise their families without the benefit of their children—who are cousins—knowing each other. You may be in a family where siblings are alienated, yet these families form the basic unit of family and community.

Summary

The story of the Promised Family runs through the life of Abraham and Sarah. The twists and turns are breathtaking. The unfolding of God's mission and purpose on the earth through the Promised Family is a strident path of consistent blessing and favor. Faith is the one ingredient for the journey of this family. Would the promise of the covenant continue without faith and obedience? The next generation will provide answers.

Questions for Reflection

1. How does the family of Abraham and Sarah resemble modern-day families?
2. What is God's purpose on the planet today, and how might your family be part of his plan?
3. What does this story tell you about families you know—next door, at work, at church, and in the community?
4. How should we respond to families that are messy and need grace?
5. What is your habit for resolving conflict in your family? How would your family's habits of conflict resolution reflect godly principles?

Chapter 5

THE PROMISED FAMILY

Isaac, Jacob, and Esau

Yes, sons are a gift from the LORD,
the fruit of the womb is a reward.

—Psalm 127:3 NET

How long should you have to wait for a promise to be fulfilled? A week, a month, a year, a decade? How about a lifetime? God always fulfills his promises but not usually in the time frame we might expect. We might not even see the fulfillment until the next generation. The story of the Promised Family continues with the next generation, which includes Abraham's son Isaac and his grandsons, Jacob and Esau. It begins with testing the faith of Abraham with the life of his promised and long-awaited son.

Testing Faith for the Promised Family

Isaac's birth brought the covenant promises into reality. The Promised Family was underway. In Genesis 22, God tested the faith of Abraham in the context of the covenant he made with Abraham. The writer of this part of the story is clear about God's intentions. God called him by name, and Abraham answered with a servant spirit saying, "Here I am."

God issued three simple imperatives to Abraham: take, go, and sacrifice (Isaac). Nothing in the story to this point could have prepared us for this strange request. You may have a sense of shock and surprise to learn God is now asking Abraham to sacrifice his promised son, the manifestation of the covenant God made with Abraham.[1] The test of Abraham is not so much focused on his obedience to God but on his faith that God will do what he has promised even if he requires the death of Isaac.[2] Human sacrifice was commonplace at that time in the land of Canaan. Yet this transaction between God and Abraham points to God's disapproval of this horrid custom.[3] Abraham obeyed immediately. Early the next morning, Abraham saddled up his donkey and took Isaac and two servants with him to the region of Moriah.

On the third day of the journey to Moriah, Abraham spotted the place where he would sacrifice Isaac and said to his servants, "Stay here with the donkey while I and the boy go over there. We will worship and then we will come back to you" (Genesis 22:5). This was clearly an act of worship as was Abraham's custom. Abraham took the gathered wood for the burnt offering for Isaac to carry while Abraham carried the fire and the knife. As they walked together, Isaac asked a question of his father. He asked, "'The fire and the wood are here,' Isaac said, 'but where is the lamb for the burnt offering?' Abraham answered, 'God himself will provide the lamb for the burnt offering, my son'" (vv. 7–8). The words for this phrase in Hebrew are *yhwh yir'eh, Jehova Jireh,* God Provides.[4] Abraham's answer to Isaac about the absence of a lamb was not intended to calm Isaac as much as a confident expression of Abraham's trust in God.[5] When they arrived at the place of sacrifice, Abraham built an altar, then bound Isaac and laid him on the altar on top of the wood (v. 9).

If Isaac was concerned for his life or unwilling to be sacrificed, he could have escaped, run away, or even overpowered Abraham. Isaac was stronger and swifter than his father.[6] He was at a time in his life when he was closest to his father, mature but not independent yet. There appears to be a touching confidence in each other, almost beyond human comprehension.[7] What is evident here on the part of Isaac is the long habit of obedience to his father. Isaac obeyed without complaint or murmur. Isaac lay on the altar in this supreme moment in his life trusting both his father and his God, putting himself at God's disposal. He took the position that his life belonged to God, that he was on this earth for God's purpose and not his own. When he was summoned to the altar of sacrifice, he did not hesitate.[8]

What did Abraham do next?

> He reached out his hand and took the knife to slay his son. But the angel of the Lord called out to him from heaven, "Abraham! Abraham!" "Here I am," he replied. "Do not lay a hand on the boy. . . . Do not do anything to him. Now I know that you fear God, because you have not withheld from me your son, your only son." (Genesis 22:10–12)

At just the right time, amid Abraham's obedience to God, he sent an angel to issue a stay of execution.[9] Abraham looked up and saw a ram caught in the thicket by its horns. Abraham went to the ram and sacrificed it instead of his son. He named "that place The Lord Will Provide. And to this day it is said, 'On the mountain of the Lord it will be provided'" (vv. 13–14).

Up to the point of drawing the knife, Abraham had no vision of substitute for his son. God was testing Abraham for a sacrifice in spirit rather than an outward act. Once Abraham demonstrated a spirit of sacrifice rather than the blood of Isaac, God's provision was disclosed. It appears that God's provision is only found on the mount and moment of sacrifice and not at any stage short of there.[10] Abraham's faith in God was the focus of this test. Obedience was required as well as a spirit of sacrifice in the context of worship. Abraham's faith and trust in God to provide is the heart of this story of the Promised Family. Isaac's willingness to trust his father and the God of his faith as a totally yielded person became part of the faith of the Promised Family.

Some theologians argue that the Abraham-Isaac story is a dramatic way of bringing about an end to child sacrifice. Kierkegaard calls this account a "suspension of the teleological" and argues that the divine will does not conform to human logic. God sets the parameters and rules in this case. Obedience does not follow the pattern of human logic and consequences. This is the Bible's way of saying God's greater good prevails.[11]

The Next Generation of the Promised Family

In chapter 23 of Genesis, Sarah passed away at the age of one hundred and twenty-seven at Kiriath Arba in the land of Canaan, the Promised Land. Abraham purchased a plot of land for four hundred shekels of silver for a field called Machpelah near Mamre. Four hundred shekels in today's dollars would be $128,000.

In Genesis 24, Abraham grew very old and began to plan for his son Isaac to find a wife from his native land of Nahor with the help of his servant. The servant traveled to the land of Nahor and found Rebekah, a suitable wife for Isaac. Rebekah traveled with her servants to Beer Lahai Roi, named "the Spring of the God who sees me" in the Negev where Isaac was living. Isaac demonstrated his love for Rebekah and married her.

Genesis 25 opens with the death of Abraham. Isaac inherited all of his father's possessions. One commentator noted that Abraham, having given gifts to the sons of his concubines, gave all his belongings to Isaac prior to his death at the age of 175 years.[12] Abraham was old and full of years as the fulfillment of what God planned. Abraham faced death with no fear.[13] Isaac and Ishmael, the sons of Abraham and Sarah, buried Abraham in the cave of Machpelah, near Mamre where Sarah was buried. The story shifts to the sons of Isaac, the promised son of the covenant God established with Abraham.

Jacob and Esau, Promised Brothers

The story of the next generation of the Promised Family comes alive with a story of brothers of the promise. "Isaac was forty years old when he married Rebekah daughter of Bethuel the Aramean from Paddan Aram and sister of Laban the Aramean. Isaac prayed to the Lord on behalf of his wife, because she was barren" (Genesis 25:20–21). The Lord answered his prayer, and Rebekah became pregnant with twins. Rebekah felt the "jostling" babies within her and asked the Lord what this meant. His answer was, "Two nations are in your womb, and two peoples from within you will be separated; one people will be stronger than the other, and the older will serve the younger" (v. 23). Esau was the firstborn of the twins and appeared hairy and reddish in color. Jacob was born next, grasping Esau's heel.

As the boys grew, Esau became a skillful hunter while Jacob became a quiet man. Since Isaac's favorite food was wild game, he favored Esau. Rebekah favored Jacob. One day Jacob was cooking stew when Esau came in from hunting, ready to eat. He told Jacob, "Quick, let me have some of that red stew! I'm famished!" Jacob took that opportunity to make a deal. He said to Esau, "First sell me your birthright." But Jacob said, "Look, I am about to die. . . . What good is the birthright to me?" Jacob insisted, "Swear to me first."

Esau agreed and Jacob gave his brother some food. Esau ate and drank and then left. He despised his birthright (Genesis 25:27–34).

It is striking, once again, that the mother of the promised covenant is barren, and that God is the one who opens the womb to bring his promise into reality. Rebekah became pregnant only after Isaac prayed to God to grant her children.[14] The barrenness of Sarah, Rebekah, Rachel, and Leah (Genesis 29:31, 35) accentuates the blessing through the chosen seed of Abraham, not accomplished through human will but through the provision of God as an act of God.[15]

Just like Abraham who had to wait a long time for the birth of Isaac, Isaac had to wait twenty years for the birth of his sons.[16] Age and time are not the determining factors in the unfolding of God's promise. Rather, it is God's will that brings his plan into reality.[17] This aspect of the story points to the requirement to be totally dependent on God, the giver of the heir of the promise.[18]

Twin brothers emerge from the same womb but are worlds apart.[19] Esau, like Ishmael, was a hunter who was at home in the open country, dissociated from mainstream society. Jacob, on the other hand, stands opposite his brother in temperament and vocation. Jacob is a quiet man. The word used to describe Jacob in Hebrew is *tam*, meaning perfect, blameless. Yet we find in this story that he is anything but blameless.[20] From the outset, we sense a conflict coming. The conflict here reflects the conflict between Cain and Abel, Isaac and Ishmael, and later with Joseph and his brothers.[21]

Even so, God's will was accomplished despite the conflict. Conflict, typically avoided, was used to bring about good. A sibling rivalry and submission will occur in the household of Jacob.[22] This sibling rivalry is accentuated by the favoritism of the parents for each child. Each parent loved and favored a different son. The word translated "love" here is *ahab*, meaning a strong preference toward one person rather than animosity toward one or the other.[23] The notion of the elder brother serving the younger brother was contrary to custom in those days, but this happened with Ishmael and Isaac as well as Esau and Jacob.[24] This issue is also in common with Cain and Abel, Rachel being chosen over Leah, and Joseph being chosen over all the rest of his brothers.

Love and preference for one child over another moves from parents to the wider family. These reversals from common custom point to God's sovereign plan of grace. The blessing was not a natural, cultural, and familial right, as a right for the firstborn son would be. God's blessing is extended and given to those who have no claim to it. They would receive what they did not earn or deserve.[25]

Birthright and Blessing

The focus at this point in this unfolding drama is on the birthright and blessing. One perspective of the birthright suggests that it gave the firstborn claim to a double share of his father's property.[26] Societies of the Ancient Near East typically recognized the eldest son by granting him privilege involving inheritance rights over the younger sons. Even though it is unclear what the birthright entailed, we know Jacob considered it something to be valued and desired.[27]

One commentator suggests the birthright may have included natural vigor of body and character, creating a presumption of success in life, a position of honor as head of the family, and perhaps a double share of the inheritance.[28] Even so, Esau seemed indifferent to his birthright and appeared to despise it.[29] Esau came in from the field famished. The original word in Hebrew is *ayep*, referring to a weakened condition due to thirst or hunger. Esau is desperate for something to eat.[30] His hunger, combined with exhaustion, puts Esau in a vulnerable position. Esau is so hungry that rather than asking for a portion to eat, chew, or taste, he asks Jacob to give him some to swallow or gulp down.[31]

Jacob saw the opportunity to make a deal. He was eager to receive his brother's birthright.[32] Jacob's response to Esau's request was swift, calculated, and spontaneous. He knew what he wanted and went after it. He came across as aggressive, dictating the terms of the transaction and spoke from a position of strength to get his hands on his brother's birthright.[33] Esau sold his birthright to his brother for a pottage of lentils.[34] In that fateful moment, Esau capitulated, and Jacob capitalized.[35] Had this been a friendly, brotherly exchange or favor, there would have been no story to record. However, Jacob knew his brother all too well and carried out his relentless purpose. He deliberately sacrificed his brother's best interest to serve himself.[36] This was Jacob's first move in deception.

After a period of famine, Isaac moved his family, including Jacob and Esau, to Gerar where Abimelech, King of the Philistines, ruled as directed by the Lord. Genesis 26 tells the story of Isaac's efforts to protect himself by representing Rebekah as his sister to King Abimelech, rather than saying Rebekah was his wife. Rebekah was beautiful and attracted the attention of Abimelech, King of the Philistines (Genesis 26:7). Isaac took the same approach as his father, Abraham, did with his mother, Sarah, who had also been beautiful and had attracted attention of Abimelech King of Gerar (20:1–17). Once again, Abimelech, King of the Philistines, discovered that Rebekah was not Isaac's sister but was his wife. He sent Isaac and Rebecca away from Gerar.

The next move is to gain control over the blessing intended for Esau. Genesis 27 records Jacob's second opportunity to take something from his brother Esau. Isaac told Esau that he was getting old and could die at any moment. He asked Esau to go into the open country and hunt wild game and prepare a tasty meal for his aging father as a prelude to giving Esau a blessing before he died.

Rebekah overheard what Isaac said to Esau. Rebekah waited for Esau to go out into the field to hunt. Once Esau left, Rebekah went to Jacob and told him what she had heard. She instructed Jacob to find two choice goats so she might prepare a meal for Isaac instead of Esau's food. She told Jacob he must do this to gain the blessing Isaac was prepared to give Esau. Rebekah prepared Jacob to present the meal to Isaac by dressing Jacob in Esau's clothes and covered in goat skins to trick his father into thinking he was Esau.

Jacob agreed to the plot, took the prepared food to his father, Isaac, dressed in Esau's clothes, including goat skins covering his arm. Isaac was deceived into thinking Jacob was Esau and proceeded to give Jacob the blessing of earth's richness, abundance of grain, new wine, nations who would serve him, lordship over his brothers, cursing for those who curse him and blessings for those who bless him. After this blessing, Jacob left Isaac's tent.

Esau arrived shortly after the blessing with the food he had prepared and asked for Isaac's blessing. Isaac was confused and asked Esau, "Who are you?" Esau responded and said, "I am your [firstborn] son."

Isaac trembled violently and said, "Who was it, then, that hunted game and brought it to me? I ate it just before you came and I blessed him—and indeed he will be blessed!"

When Esau heard his father's words, he burst out with a loud and bitter cry and said to his father, "Bless me—me too, my father!"

But he said, "Your brother came deceitfully and took your blessing."

Esau said, ". . . He has deceived me these two times: He took my birthright, and now he's taken my blessing!" (Genesis 27:32–36)

Rather than a blessing, Isaac told Esau he would not live with earth's richness, away from the dew of heaven, and that he would live by the sword and serve his younger brother (vv. 39–40), Esau wept aloud and held a grudge against his brother Jacob. He vowed to wait until his father died to then kill Jacob. When Rebekah heard of Esau's plans to kill Jacob, she instructed Jacob to flee to Haran and stay with her brother Laban until Esau's fury subsided (vv. 41–46).

There is a clear moral lapse in the parenting approach of Isaac and Rebekah. Yet God maintains his commitment to Abraham's clan despite the declining solidarity of the family to whom the covenant promise was given.[37] The story of Jacob and Esau reveals the depth of hostility and bitterness between these brothers.[38] Rebekah and Jacob became coconspirators with offensive action that fractures the family for two decades and contributes to the disgrace of Jacob throughout history. Rebekah dupes her husband and wrongs both of her sons in the process.[39] One commentator suggested Rebekah was living up to the oracle that the elder will serve the younger by favoring Jacob.[40]

In the folly of this drama, no one seems to be concerned or focused on the promise made to Abraham.[41] Rather, Rebekah took matters into her own hands. When she realized Isaac was planning to bless Esau, the elder brother, she injected her skillful management and saw no other way of fulfilling God's purpose and Jacob's rights than by her interference.[42] Rebekah became the prime manipulator, controlling the direction of action by overhearing Isaac's intent. Aware of Isaac's intent to bless Esau, she devised a scheme to intervene.[43]

Jacob and Rebekah gained nothing by their interference in God's plan and lost a great deal in the process. God has already promised the birthright would be Jacob's. The mother lost her son. Jacob had to flee for his life and most likely never saw his mother again. Jacob lost all the comforts of home and all the possessions his father accumulated.[44] Esau was angry and developed a grudge for his brother Jacob. The word *grudge, satam* in Hebrew, means a deep-seated anger that results in violent retaliation.[45] Rebekah underestimated the consequences of her action. She thought Jacob would be away for a while. That "while" turned into twenty years.[46]

Over time, Jacob the deceiver is deceived by Laban in the giving of his firstborn daughter, Leah, in marriage, according to local custom. Then after Jacob provided labor for seven more years, Laban allowed Jacob to marry Rachel, the one he loved (29:14–30). Jacob was blessed as his father pronounced but struggled with Laban, his father-in-law. He had to flee for his life again (31:1–55). Jacob and Laban finally reconciled, but Jacob wrestled with God and finally prepared to meet his brother Esau. Jacob humbly bowed before his brother in fear and bore gifts for him. The two reconciled and went on their way (33:1–16).

Even with all the human interference, mean deception, slyness, blundering unbelief, and profane worldliness of the human transaction between family members, God's truth and mercy find a way.[47] Through the pain of loss, deceit, and conflict, God continued to deliver on the promise he made to Abraham, to Isaac, and now to Jacob as part of the Promised Family.

Principles for Family Hope

There are numerous principles for modern-day families to apply from the experience of the next generation of the Promised Family including Isaac, Rebekah, Jacob, and Esau. The principles for family hope are listed under the following categories:

Family Blessing. Are God's promises reliable? God alone is the source of all blessing and favor. He chose to bless all the families of the world through Abram, including yours and mine. God wants to bless your family, and he wants to bless other families through your family. Families who find faith in the God of Abram will be blessed. The blessings God has in store for your family will be an avalanche of blessing to your family and your children. Through faith in Jesus, we are redeemed and are useful in God's redemptive work in history. We become agents of redemption, participating in God's plan of redemption. Your family is blessed to be a blessing.

Promised Blessing. What does God expect from us once he has made a promise to us for our lives? God promises to bless us, and he keeps his promises. God promised Abram what seemed from a human point of view to be an impossible promise—but not impossible with God. The time line for God's blessing is not always what we might imagine, but it will come, nevertheless. The hardest part of receiving God's promise of blessing is waiting for it. The waiting requires faith and trust in God and his word. In the meantime, we must adapt our ways of living and wait on the Lord and his promise.

Family Life Is Hard. What alternatives do we have when our culture conflicts with God's word? The experiences of living in a family can be exceedingly difficult. There may be experiences that bring no present comfort or peace. Instead, they may lead to crushing trouble or anxiety or an unsatisfied craving.[48] Yet the believer and his or her family must hold on in faith and expect God to provide an answer. This is God's way of educating us and helping us learn how to loosen our hold on temporal things to focus on what is spiritual and real.

Respect and Dignity. What does this story teach us about how we treat other people? Treating all people with respect and dignity is a critical principle of relating to others. Sarai treated Hagar as though she was less human rather than as a woman with hopes and dreams. Sarai inflicted deep pain on Hagar. There is never an excuse to treat another human being, one made in God's image, with anything less than respect and dignity.

Human Solutions. God does not need help fulfilling his promises. When we provide human solutions to promises that appear to be beyond our own timetable, we only invite trouble and make things worse. Trying to manage the consequences of our poor decisions only complicates the matter.

God Sees Your Family. Regardless of how difficult your family situation might be, despite your sense of feeling alone, abandoned, and forgotten, remember that God sees you and your family. God is in your life. He has not lost track of you. He knows where you are, he sees you, and he hears your misery. You are not alone.

God's Purpose and Plan. God has a purpose for you and your family. Your sense of aloneness has not diminished God's plan for you and your family. His plan is real, and so is your life. We find our purpose in life by submitting to God rather than running away. When we feel insignificant, ousted from our natural place in the world's households, God has a place for us. When we lose our way in life, we are not out of his view. Even when we do not think of choosing him, his divine and all-embracing love chooses us.[49] Our response should be to trust and obey him.

Families in Crisis Need Support. All families will face crises like the situations experienced by Abraham, Isaac, Jacob, and Esau. Families are usually not prepared for crisis, illness, displacement, conflict, economic loss, death, and an array of other unfortunate situations. Families may experience loss, pain, grief, calamity, separation, joblessness, homelessness, abuse, trauma, divorce, and disintegration. Families are human, therefore imperfect. They live in a fallen world and often face difficult circumstances. Families need critical and timely support when a crisis comes. They also need to know where God is through the deep and dark valleys of life. They need to be reminded of God's presence and his promises in difficult times.

Churches, nonprofit ministries, and counseling ministries are in the best position to provide family care when crisis comes.

Summary

The story of the next generation of the Promised Family runs through the lives of Isaac, Jacob, and Esau. Family strife and conflict invade the lives of the next generation. Issues of parenting, sibling rivalry, and favoritism plague these families. Yet God is faithful to bless these families and carry out his purpose and promise through them. How would the blessings and promises of the covenant show up in the families to come? Family dysfunction and conflict emerge in the story of Joseph and his brothers. How will the tragedy of sibling rivalry and mistreatment factor into God's redemptive plan for the people Israel? The next chapter provides answers to these questions.

Questions for Reflection

1. How do the families of Isaac, Jacob, and Esau resemble modern-day families?
2. How can your family with its own uniqueness be a part of God's plan in human history?
3. How do the stories of these families compare to families you know today?
4. How might your family serve families who struggle with conflict?
5. How does your family resolve conflict?

Chapter 6

THE REDEEMING FAMILY

Joseph and His Brothers

How good and pleasant it is when brothers live together in unity!

—Psalm 133:1

If your family is like every other human family, it has its share of imperfections, faults, mishaps, betrayals, and perhaps even tragedies. Through God's grace and desire to redeem our families, he provides a way for us to overcome challenges and our own imperfections. In other words, God has the power to take our sinful behavior, even in families, and turn it into something beautiful. All families need redemption at some level. The hard work of forgiveness after an offense and reconciliation after a period of estrangement is the core work of God's love and grace.

You will see these truths for families illustrated in the lives of the Redeeming Family—Joseph and his brothers. The biblical record of their story begins in Genesis 37. Jacob made peace with his brother, Esau, and settled in the land of Canaan. Joseph, one of Jacob's sons, a seventeen-year-old, was assigned to tend the flocks with his brothers. Jacob loved Joseph more than any of his other sons because he had been born to him in his old age.

Jacob, also known as Israel, made a richly ornamental robe for Joseph to wear, which set the stage for brotherly conflict.[1] His brothers took note of the special robe and knew their father loved Joseph more than he loved them. Their response was hatred for their brother Joseph, and they were unable to bring themselves to speak a kind word to him. This is the same type of rage that Cain had toward Abel.[2] To make things worse, Joseph had a dream in which his brothers all bowed down to him. Joseph relayed this dream to his brothers, which caused them to hate him even more. Their hatred turned into jealousy and a plot to kill him. Rather than kill him, though, Joseph's brothers bound him, threw him into a well, and sold him as a slave to a caravan of Ishmaelites headed for Egypt. Joseph was taken to Egypt as a slave and was bought by Potiphar, an Egyptian official and captain of the guard (Genesis 37). God blessed everything Joseph did while he served Potiphar and was promoted to household manager running all the affairs of Potiphar's house.

Sentenced to Prison

Potiphar's wife noticed Joseph was handsome and tried to seduce him for sexual relations. Joseph refused her advances in honor of Potiphar, his master. Potiphar's wife then accused Joseph of sexual advances and complained to Potiphar about this incident. Potiphar, filled with anger, threw Joseph in prison, where he served under the warden's supervision. The Lord blessed the work of Joseph's hands and gave him success in everything he did. The warden placed everything under Joseph's supervision (Genesis 39). During Joseph's time in prison, Pharaoh's baker and cupbearer offended him and were thrown into prison with Joseph. Both men had dreams while in prison that Joseph was able to interpret. However, the cupbearer did not remember Joseph's ability to interpret dreams (Genesis 40).

From the Prison to the Palace

Two years after the cupbearer was released from prison, Pharaoh had two troubling dreams. He convened his magicians and wise men to gain the meaning of these dreams, but they were unable to interpret them for him. Finally, the cupbearer was reminded of Joseph and told Pharaoh of his ability to interpret dreams.

Pharaoh sent for Joseph to be brought from the dungeon in prison. Pharaoh told Joseph his dreams and asked for an interpretation. Joseph said, "I cannot do it . . . but God will give Pharaoh the answer he desires" (41:16). Joseph remarked that both dreams were one and the same. He interpreted the dreams as God telling Pharaoh he was going to send seven seasons of plentiful harvests followed by seven seasons of drought and famine in the land. In addition to interpreting the dreams, Joseph recommended a plan to respond to the revelation of God about the seasons of harvest and the seasons of famine by appointing commissioners and someone to manage the harvest and save grain for the lean years.

Pharaoh appointed Joseph to oversee his palace and the plan he outlined for the years of harvest and drought. Joseph was promoted to second in command of the land of Egypt (41:40), and he was equipped with Pharaoh's signet ring, robes of fine linen, a gold chain, and a chariot. Pharaoh decreed that "without your word no one will lift hand or foot in all of Egypt" (v. 44). Pharaoh gave Joseph the name Zaphenath-Paneah and gave him Asenath, the daughter of Potiphera the priest of On, to be his wife (v. 45).

The famine predicted in Pharaoh's dream came to pass, and none of the nations around Egypt had any food. However, Egypt had plenty of food due to the management of the harvest during the years of plenty. Joseph oversaw this plan and began selling food to neighboring nations who had nothing to eat.

Joseph's Brothers Head to Egypt

Joseph's brothers and his father were living in Canaan, where drought and famine were severe. They heard there was food in Egypt and decided to travel there to buy grain. Jacob sent ten of his sons to buy grain but did not allow Benjamin, the youngest, to go. Since Joseph was the official who oversaw selling grain, his ten brothers appeared before him and bowed down in his presence, just as Joseph dreamed years before. Joseph recognized his brothers, but they did not recognize him. He pretended not to recognize them and spoke harshly to them and accused them of being spies. They rejected that claim and said they only came to buy grain to eat. Joseph insisted his brothers were spies and required them to return home with grain and bring back Benjamin, their youngest brother. Simeon agreed to stay in prison while the other nine brothers traveled back to Canaan to return with their youngest brother. When they arrived home, they realized their money had been returned to them (42:28, 35). Joseph instructed his brothers to return with Benjamin on their return trip to Egypt. However, Jacob, their father resisted this requirement (v. 38).

Second Trip to Egypt

After Jacob and his sons had eaten all the grain they brought home from Egypt, Jacob sent them back to Egypt to buy more food. This time, with Benjamin, they presented themselves before Joseph again but still did not recognize him. When Joseph saw his brothers, he ordered his servants to slaughter an animal and prepare a meal for him to share with his brothers. The brothers were frightened because they thought they were summoned to Joseph's house because of the returned silver.

When Joseph joined his brothers for the meal, he asked how their father was. But Joseph was so deeply moved by the sight of

Benjamin that he hurried out of the room to a private room to weep. After regaining control of himself, Joseph came out and ordered the servants to serve the food (Genesis 43). After the meal, Joseph ordered his servants to pack the mules of his brothers with as much grain as they could carry and a bag of silver in each bag. He then instructed them to place Joseph's silver cup into Benjamin's bag. On their journey home, the brothers realized what had happened when they were approached by Egyptian guards and taken back to Egypt. Joseph demanded that the holder of his silver cup stay with him as a prisoner while the rest of the brothers returned to Canaan (Genesis 44). But the drama of the moment overwhelmed Joseph.

Joseph Reveals Himself to His Brothers

When Joseph could no longer contain himself, he cried out, "Have everyone leave my presence!" (45:1). Joseph was left alone with his brothers when he revealed himself. He cried so loudly that the Egyptians heard it and Pharaoh's household heard about it as well. He told his brothers, "I am Joseph! Is my father still living?" (v. 3). His brothers were not able to answer him because they were terrified at his presence. "Joseph said to his brothers, 'Come close to me. . . . I am your brother Joseph, the one you sold into Egypt! And now, do not be distressed and do not be angry with yourselves for selling me here, because it was to save lives that God sent me ahead of you. . . . So then, it was not you who sent me here, but God'" (vv. 4–8).

Joseph discouraged his brothers from feeling remorse over their actions.[3] All of Egypt became enslaved to Joseph and under his control, except his own family, but Joseph refused to take advantage of their vulnerability.[4] Joseph hugged and kissed Benjamin, and he kissed all his brothers and spoke with them. He encouraged them to go and get their father and return to Egypt where he was planning for them to live in Goshen (Genesis 45).

When Pharaoh learned Joseph's brothers had arrived in Egypt, he was very pleased and planned for them to move to Egypt to join Joseph. Jacob, at the age of 130, and his sons returned to Egypt to live in the land of Goshen as Joseph suggested (47:9). Seventeen years after Jacob arrived in Egypt, he took time to bless all his sons. He died shortly after the giving of the blessing at the age of 147 (47:28–49:33). Joseph threw himself on his father and wept over him and kissed him. He made plans to embalm his father and transport him to the land of Canaan to bury him as Jacob requested.

Revenge or Redemption

The death of Jacob was cause for concern among Joseph's brothers because they feared revenge (50:15). They were unsure of what their future held given their past treatment of Joseph, and their father's death aroused a deep sense of anxiety and guilt.[5] They gathered and sent word to Joseph in the form of a letter saying, "Your father left these instructions before he died; 'This is what you are to say to Joseph: I ask you to forgive your brothers the sins and the wrongs they committed in treating you so badly.' Now please forgive the sins of the servants of the God of your father." One commentator pointed out the effort at self-preservation (suggesting the letter of instruction was fake) and the effort to present themselves as slaves to Joseph.[6]

When their message came to Joseph, he wept. His brothers came and threw themselves down before Joseph again and said, "'We are your slaves,' they said. But Joseph said to them, 'Don't be afraid. Am I in the place of God? You intended to harm me, but God intended it for good to accomplish what is now being done, the saving of many lives. So then, don't be afraid. I will provide for you and your children.'" Joseph immediately encouraged his brothers to not be afraid.[7] Instead, he reassured them and spoke kindly to them (Genesis 50:15–21).

Joseph's forgiveness arose from his commitment to God.[8] In addition, Joseph promised to continue to care for his brothers and their families. He became his family's keeper long after the famine.[9] In other words, Joseph is saying that God has already spoken on this matter.[10] Behind the scenes, God continued to work out his unchanging plan, his good plan.[11] Joseph's forgiveness of his brothers demonstrated his acceptance of God's providential care, which included his brothers' evil deed. The brotherly love became an expression of humble gratitude for the mystery of divine providence.[12] Joseph viewed the entire ordeal through the lens of God's providence and as part of God's overall plan of salvation for the descendants of Israel.[13]

The twelve sons of Israel experienced divine grace that superseded the temptations of murder and vengeance that would have threatened the promissory blessing.[14] God is seen as the redeemer of those who have been cast off and cast aside. He is also the one who matures Joseph through suffering and humiliation, which enables him to forgive his brothers. The story shows how the human family overcomes deception, jealousy, hatred, and even murder, perhaps an allusion to Cain. The account of Joseph and his brothers also demonstrates that the family is resilient, reliable, and redeemable. Success and failure in families becomes a requisite of God's larger plan.[15] Joseph becomes the exemplar for forgiveness and reconciliation. In the end, there is the promise of restored relationships with both God and human siblings.[16] Joseph lived in peace with his brothers and lived to be one hundred and ten years of age.

Principles for Family Hope

The story of the Redeeming Family demonstrates how family life and the experience of siblings can be messy, almost to the point of no return. Yet, in the messiness of family life, God continues to work out his plan in redemptive history. He redeems the family of Joseph while overcoming the human errors of parenting and sibling rivalry. Here are a few lessons we can apply.

Favoritism Sets the Stage for Conflict. The natural yet unfortunate consequences of selecting a favorite child from among siblings and treating that child in unique ways is foundational for sibling conflict and rivalry. Parents should do everything in their power to love and treat each child as a valued member of the family.

God's Favor Aligns with His Plan. On the other hand, God chooses to favor and bless his children, his chosen people. It appears from Joseph's story that God favors and blesses us with success through skills and abilities so that they ultimately align with his plan of salvation and redemption. Wherever Joseph landed, even due to unjust treatment, God continued to favor and bless everything Joseph did. Learn to celebrate the successes, the strengths, and the abilities of your children. God may be shaping them for a future use in his redemptive plan.

Principled Living. Joseph refused the seduction of Potiphar's wife. It would have been unthinkable to dishonor the trust of his master and his relationship to God, who sent him to serve in Potiphar's house. Your children will always be secure in God's hands even amid unjust treatment. Joseph learned these basic principles of ethical living from his father and mother. However, Joseph's mother, Rachel, died young, shortly after the birth of Benjamin. She held on to the gods of her father (31:19) and may not have provided the kind of spiritual guidance and faith of Jacob. Parents should take every opportunity to invest the Word of God into the lives, hearts, and minds of their children. These early lessons will serve to guide them when they must make decisions without parental guidance.

Audience of One. Whether Joseph was assigned to Potiphar's house, the prison, or the palace, he learned to live for and serve an audience of one: God. No earthly authority or situation was greater than his personal relationship and devotion to God. Parents must make every effort to impress the omniscient and omnipresent character of God. Children will gain confidence and an awareness of the presence of God that will guide them toward right living. They will learn how to be a person of faith in the darkness and in the limelight.

The Power of Forgiveness. One of the most critical habits to learn is the ability to forgive those who have harmed, hurt, and injured you. Teach this to your children, especially with siblings. Point to God as the ultimate example of forgiveness. Teach them how God in Christ has forgiven us for our sins and seeks to restore us and realign us to his purpose. Lead your children and your family to have a God-consciousness about life, relationships, and spiritual matters. This ability is foundational to healthy, God-honoring family life. Conflict is inevitable. Forgiveness is a choice that leads to reconciliation in family relationships.

God Redeems. All families are fallen, broken, and sinful. No family is perfect. Even the best families, the families God uses in his plan of redemption are flawed and less than what they could be. Yet our family brokenness is the perfect laboratory in which to experience God's grace, mercy, and redeeming power. What he allows, he also redeems. Teach your children to know and learn about God the Redeemer. This one truth will serve them in the dark days of life. Teach them to put their faith in God, despite the hard places in life.

Summary

The transition of Joseph and his brothers and their families meant their salvation and rescue. The redemption made available in the land of Egypt became the land of captivity as the nation of Israel was subjected to harsh treatment and slavery as the nation grew. The need for a liberator arose, and two mothers demonstrated incredible impact and influence in the making of a leader named Moses.

Questions for Reflection

1. How can parents create a family environment with no favorites among siblings?
2. What are the best ways to teach children how to forgive?
3. After forgiveness, what does it take to reconcile relationships in the family?
4. What are some examples of forgiveness in the Bible you can share with your children?
5. What do we say about ourselves when we choose a grudge over grace?

Chapter 7

THE LIBERATING FAMILY

Moses and His Mothers

A mother's love is the fuel that enables a normal
human being to do the impossible.

—Marion C. Garretty

Amother's work is endless. Her concern for her children extends
beyond childhood into adult years. The labor of love of mothers is a powerful source of influence and liberation. A mother who
knows the Lord also knows her child was created with a divine purpose. Mothers with a faith relationship with the Lord work tirelessly
to free their children to become all that God intended. They liberate
their children to fulfill their destiny in God's redemptive plan. This
chapter tells the story of how three women were used to save a baby
from death. There are two mothers and two daughters, with the
daughter of Pharaoh in two roles—initially that of daughter and
eventually also an adoptive mother.[1] The mothers in Moses's life
played a key role in the future liberation of the nation of Israel.

The story of Moses and his family begins at the closing of the
book of Genesis. Joseph was taken in captivity to Egypt, promoted
to the second in command, and later received his brothers and father
there to save their lives during a famine that swept the region. The

people of Israel survived the famine while in Egypt but over time were enslaved by Egyptian rulers and in need of a leader who would liberate them from bondage. Moses became that leader. At the beginning of the book of Exodus, the writer records the arrival of the sons of Jacob in Egypt, including Reuben, Simeon, Levi, Judah, Issachar, Zebulun, Benjamin, Dan, Naphtali, Gad, and Asher. Their families came with them, and Joseph was already in Egypt. Joseph and all his brothers died, but the people of Israel rapidly multiplied and filled the land of Egypt.

A new pharaoh came to power who did not know Joseph and his role in saving the nation from drought and famine. The new pharaoh was concerned by the growth of the Israelite people and ordered slave masters to put them to work through forced labor in building projects for the store cities of Pithom and Rameses (Exodus 1:1–14). These store cities, located in the northeastern part of Egypt, were built to provide provisions for Egyptian troops. The descendants of Joseph and his brothers were subjected to harsh labor and were used ruthlessly by the Egyptians, yet the Israelites continued to grow in number.

Egyptian Abortion

The pharaoh of Egypt feared the expansion of the Israelites and instructed Hebrew midwives, Shiphrah and Puah, to observe the birth of Hebrew babies. If the baby was a girl, she was allowed to live, but if the baby was a boy, the midwife was to kill the Hebrew baby boy. However, the midwives, who feared God, did not do what the king ordered. When questioned about why they allowed the Hebrew babies to live, they answered, "Hebrew women are not like Egyptian women; they are vigorous and give birth before the midwives arrive." In desperation Pharaoh gave this order to all his people: "Every boy that is born you must throw into the Nile, but let every girl live" (Exodus 1:15–22). Pharaoh decided the only way to curb the Hebrew population was to kill all baby boys by throwing them into the Nile River. This is the context into which Moses, the liberator, was born.

The Birth of Moses

Moses hails from the house of Levi, one of Jacob's sons who settled in the land of Egypt. A man from the house of Levi married a Levite woman, who became pregnant and gave birth to a son (Exodus 2:1–2). When Moses's mother, Jochebed, saw him, she recognized that he was a fine child, a good child. In an age of high infant mortality, abandoning a healthy child would have been a bitter experience.[2] Immediately after Moses's birth, Jochebed hid him for three months. She did what any responsible, caring mother would have done: love her baby and try to keep him alive.[3]

After three months, the baby became too active, too loud to hide any longer. Jochebed cleverly decided to put her son in the one place no Egyptian would bother to look: the Nile River itself, exactly where Hebrew baby boys were supposed to be cast (Exodus 2:3).[4] Jochebed obeyed Pharaoh's decree in her own way. She "puts" (*sam*) rather than "throws" (*hislik*) the boy into the Nile. She places him, not into the middle of the Nile, but among the rushes near the shore.[5] In a sense, Jochebed complied with Pharaoh's command but with a twist of her own.[6]

The absence of action on the part of Moses's father, Amram, should not be misconstrued as disinterest or disfavor. The writer of Hebrews makes it clear that "By faith, Moses' parents hid him for three months after he was born, because they saw he was no ordinary child, and they were not afraid of the king's edict" (Hebrews 11:23). Rather, the Exodus description focused more on the mother's role. Amram would have been expected to labor as a slave away from the household for long hours daily. Jochebed was the one who had to carry out the risky and innovative preservation plan for her son.[7]

Noah's Ark 2.0

Jochebed took a papyrus basket and coated it with tar and pitch. She then took the basket and put it among the reeds along the bank of the Nile where Egyptian soldiers were not likely to look for a newborn. The pitch she used was made of various sorts of tar mixtures and tarry substances. She may have been influenced by the Legend of Sargon of Akkad, in which Sargon was placed into a river in a container made of reeds sealed with pitch, rescued by a water-drawer, cared for, and raised. He eventually became a legendary hero and then king. She may have also been influenced by the Genesis flood story in some form with its own parallels of rescue on water in a pitch-sealed container.

Moses's sister, Miriam, stood at a distance from the basket to see what would happen to her baby brother. The involvement of Miriam demonstrates that the family was involved in protecting Moses, as would be expected.[8] Jochebed clearly had something in mind besides child abandonment. Each action she took was full of love and hope of deliverance even though the specifics could not have been known to her.[9] What happened next appears to have surprised everyone involved.

The Discovery of Moses

Pharaoh's daughter went down to the Nile to bathe with her attendants. As they walked along the banks of the river, she saw a basket among the reeds and asked her slave girl to go and get it. She opened the basket, saw the baby crying, and felt sorry for him. She said, "This is one of the Hebrew babies." There is no suggestion that Moses's basket was placed where the Egyptians might have found it.

To the contrary, this was not part of the plan Jochebed envisioned. For an Egyptian to discover Moses would have meant putting the baby in harm's way.[10]

Moses's sister, Miriam, asked Pharaoh's daughter, "Shall I go and get one of the Hebrew women to nurse the baby for you?" Pharaoh's daughter said yes, so Miriam went and brought the baby's actual mother. Pharaoh's daughter said to Moses's mother, "'Take this baby and nurse him for me, and I will pay you.' So the woman took the baby and nursed him" (Exodus 2:9).

During these days of nursing and raising Moses, Jochebed and Amram had their opportunity to teach him all they knew about the God of his fathers.[11] Moses must have grown up hearing the story of his discovery from his adoptive mother, his biological mother, and his sister.[12] Jochebed was delivered from a prison of fear to the security of being paid to nurse her own son.[13] She did everything she could to prevent her son's death and ended up being able to nurse and rear her own little boy.[14] It must have been difficult for her to process the fact that an Egyptian woman, the enemy, found the son she was trying to hide.

God turned unimaginable circumstances into hope and salvation.[15] Moses was delivered from the condemnation of grinding slavery to enjoying the best of both worlds.[16] He was treated with maternal kindness by the daughter of the pharaoh who had condemned him to death. She also entrusted his care to the one woman in all the world who wanted the best for him.[17] There is a bit of humor in that Pharaoh's daughter hired Moses's mother to do the very thing she wanted to do for her son.[18] But Moses needed a family in which to grow and develop.

The Adoption of Moses

In ancient times, children were nursed until they were three or four years of age, so the Egyptian princess did not gain custody of

Moses until he was older.[19] After he was weaned, Moses's mother took him to Pharaoh's daughter, and he became her son. "She named him Moses, saying, 'I drew him out of the water'" (2:10). The Egyptian princess consciously honored Moses's Hebrew origins and made him legitimately Egyptian with a name in her own language, emphasizing she was adopting a son.[20] The motives of Moses's mother, Miriam his sister, and Pharaoh's daughter appear to have been pure and appropriate. Even though Moses grew up in Pharaoh's household, there is evidence that he grew up knowing his sister, Miriam, and his brother, Aaron, since he later said to Jethro, his father-in-law, "Let me go back to my own people in Egypt to see if any of them are still alive" (4:18). God used these women to do what they were good at doing and what their culture especially honored in women: preserving and raising a child.[21]

Through God's divine providence, Jochebed was hired to nurse her own son and nurture him as a child. Moses had the motherly love and care every child needs and wants. She was able to teach Moses about Hebrew life, culture, and faith, as well as orient him to the God of Israel. Miriam was instrumental in connecting Jochebed to Pharaoh's daughter to nurse her newfound son. Miriam was at the right place at the right time to make this connection for her brother Moses. Pharaoh's daughter adopted Moses as her son and raised him according to the culture, customs, and civic responsibilities of Pharaoh's family. These women played a foundational role in preparing Moses to liberate a nation.

Liberating a Nation

Moses grew up as an Egyptian young leader. He began to witness the mistreatment of his people, the Israelites, at the hands of Egyptian soldiers. He took the liberation of his people into his own hands and murdered an Egyptian soldier who was mistreating an

Israelite and hid his body in the sand. When Moses realized his countrymen had seen the murder, he feared for his life and fled to the land of Midian in the desert (Exodus 2:11–15).

Moses settled in the land of Midian and married Zipporah, the daughter of Jethro. While he was tending the flock of Jethro, the Lord appeared to Moses through a burning bush and called him to lead the people of Israel out of bondage. His task was to go to Pharaoh and tell him to release the people of Israel from bondage (Exodus 3). Moses doubted his ability and pleaded with the Lord to send someone else. But God insisted that Moses was the right man for the job.

Moses returned to Egypt and asked Pharaoh to release the people of Israel, but Pharaoh refused to free them. In return, the Lord told Moses he was going to send plagues to Egypt. Moses warned Pharaoh, but Pharaoh hardened his heart toward God. God sent the plagues of blood in the water, gnats in the sky, flies, the death of livestock, hail, locusts, darkness, and finally the death of the firstborn (Exodus 4–11). Moses then led the people of Israel to prepare for what would come to be known as the Passover, to avoid the impact of the angel of death on the firstborn of Israel (Exodus 12). After these plagues and the death of Pharaoh's firstborn son, he finally agreed to let the people of Israel begin the exodus out of Egypt and into the desert.

The people of Israel, their children, grandchildren, and all their possessions were loaded in a caravan and headed for the desert. They came to the Red Sea and were trapped with Pharaoh's army in pursuit. God opened the waters of the Red Sea, allowed for the crossing of the Israelite people, and then closed the waters on the Egyptian army and destroyed them by drowning (Exodus 13–14).

The people of Israel were finally free from their oppressors and wandered in the desert for forty years until they reached the Promised Land (Exodus 16–40). In the desert, Moses received the Ten

Commandments and led the people to the edge of the land of Canaan. But Moses was not allowed to enter the Promised Land. Nevertheless, he was the instrumental leader who led the people of Israel out of bondage and to the edge of the land promised to Abraham.

The Influence of Mothers

You may have heard the adage "The hand that rocks the cradle rules the world." The point of this chapter is to focus on the role and influence of a mother. One cannot underestimate the impact of Moses's mothers on his life and leadership. The love of Moses's mothers enabled him to do the impossible: to rise to the call of God to liberate a nation. Moses's mother and his adoptive mother had an incredible influence on the life and trajectory of Moses as a leader, liberator, and shepherd of a nation.

The women in Moses's life not only contributed to the prospering of the children of Israel but enabled this particular child, destined to become Israel's leader, to emerge with the best possible preparation for his task.[22] The wisdom writer of the book of Proverbs recorded a litany of characteristics of women, wives, and mothers that point us to the kind of women who shape the world. In Proverbs 31, she is described as a woman of noble character, one who carries the full confidence of her husband, brings her family good all the days of her life, works with eager hands, and provides food for her family (Proverbs 31:10–15). She is seen as a woman of strength and compared to a lioness in the care of her young.[23] As a lioness, she puts the well-being of her household before her own comfort.[24] She is engaged in real estate, agribusiness, commerce, and works late into the night for the benefit of her family (Proverbs 31:16–19). These activities are occasional,[25] yet there is a strain of industry that runs through her blood.[26] She is a manager of the household and a person of commerce.[27] She demonstrates great strength, prowess, and ingenuity and would seem to commend the extraordinary ability of a wife in providing for her household even against great odds.[28] Her home is her base of operations in the community where she serves the poor and needy.[29] She provides clothes for her family, furnishings for her home, and is clothed in fine linen. She keeps a sharp lookout over the affairs of her household and is ready to right any irregularities to maintain its orderly arrangement.[30] She is respected in the city and takes her place among the leaders of the land.

This admirable woman is clothed with strength and dignity and knows the value of humor. She speaks with wisdom and faithful instruction (Proverbs 31:20–27). This wise wife is the mediator of Yahweh's blessings to the house. It is through her work and her "fear of Yahweh" that *shalom*, peace, prevails.[31] She is known as a wise and gracious teacher.[32] The ancient sages believed that a woman like this with strength, determination, skill, diligence, devotion, and cleverness provided the foundation for the success of her family and the success of her community.[33]

One commentator said, "What the homes of a nation are, the nation is; and it is woman's high and beautiful function to make the homes, and within her power lies the terrible capacity for marring them."[34] Therefore, it follows that the condition of a woman is the touchstone for civilized society.[35] Mothers who condition their sons to search for these kinds of qualities in a wife will teach them to avoid pursuing superficial beauties and vanishing charms in the women they choose.[36] The children of the Proverbs 31 Woman respect her and call her blessed. Her husband praises her. While she is beautiful, the inner beauty she carries is her fear of the Lord. She should be rewarded for what she has earned and should be praised in public (Proverbs 31:28–31). These are the kinds of women who are to be praised.

I think of the women in my life—my mother, Gloria Garcia Reyes; my mother-in-law, Elia Olivares Alvarado; and my wife,

Belinda Alvarado Reyes. I have been blessed beyond any expectation because they brightly reflect the Proverbs 31 woman. They have profoundly shaped me and have enabled me to become the man I am today. They have shaped their husbands, sons, and daughters with the fear of the Lord and have demonstrated the characteristics of the type of woman that shapes a home and a nation.

Principles for Family Hope

The story of Moses is one powerful example of how a biological mother and an adoptive mother both shaped a national leader, a nation, and a future destiny of a people within the context of God's redemptive work in history. Here are some principles to consider about the value of mothers.

Fear and Obey the Lord. Above all, the Hebrew midwives feared and obeyed the Lord God more than Pharaoh. They did so at the risk of their own lives. They thought it was more important to obey God than to obey man. The Lord blessed these midwives with children of their own and protected them from harm. Mothers who fear the Lord and obey his commands above all will be blessed and honored by the Lord. This is the one quality that sets godly mothers apart. Their work harmonizes into the redemptive work of God in human history.

Courage, Innovation, and Faith. Jochebed demonstrated a great deal of courage and ingenuity when she developed a plan to indirectly comply with Pharaoh's edict while also finding a way to preserve her son's life. She worked out a solution by faith that her son was to be preserved rather than abandoned. Sometimes we can only do what we know to do and depend on God for a way out of a bad situation. Mothers solve problems, but they are wise when they depend on the Lord for help too. Mothers with courage, innovation, and faith can shape the future of a nation.

Space for God to Work. Mothers filled with faith always leave room for God to work in supernatural and surprising ways in their children's lives. Wise mothers do not try to take the place of God in their children's lives. Rather, they recognize the sovereignty of God, the power of God, to intervene and depend on God to engage at the right time. They recognize the plans and purpose of God in their children's lives and are open to his intervention. Jochebed did not plan for Moses to be discovered by an Egyptian princess, but God did. This is how God works in the lives of our children—that is, in unexpected and surprising ways that demonstrate again he alone is God. His ways are not our ways. His thoughts are not our thoughts (Isaiah 55:8).

Forever Families. The best place for a child to grow and develop is in a family. This was true for Moses even though he did not grow up entirely in his biological family. His biological family was nearby and close enough to serve him. Yet his adoptive mother, the daughter of Pharaoh, became his family until he was a young man. Adoptive families fill the gap when living with one's biological family is not possible. They are heroic families for children who need a home in which to flourish. God provided not only an adoptive family for Moses but also the financial resources for Jochebed to nurse him in his early years. Where God guides, he also provides.

The High Calling. Being a mother is a high calling in life. Mothers shape boys and girls who will become men and women who will shape a community, a village, a city, a state, and a nation. This role in society stabilizes a community of people. The training school of the home is where we learn how to live, how to get along with others, how to respect, and how to treat others as we want to be treated. We learn how to love, forgive, lead, organize, and share with others in the home. Mothers are critically strategic in the shaping of leaders and nations.

The Home, Microcosm of the Nation. The well-being of the home managed well by its mother reflects the nation. The well-being of mothers is the responsibility of men and the entire family. Every society, village, and community are made up of families, of homes that comprise the community. The health of the home will be the health of the community. When families succeed, communities succeed. The opposite is also true.

Celebrate Women. A wise and godly woman is to be celebrated. She must be afforded every opportunity to learn, excel, thrive, lead, and be affirmed for her incredible work in and outside the home. Women who are enterprising, commerce oriented, providers in the home, and respected in the city are to be celebrated by other women and especially by the children and men in their lives. They are to be praised.

Summary

Liberation from Egypt freed the people of Israel from bondage and sent them on their way to the land God promised to Abraham, Isaac, and Jacob. As the nation grew, so did their desire to be like other nations who had kings. What would family life be like for the ruler of Israel? Those answers emerge in the next chapter.

Questions for Reflection

1. What are the most desirable characteristics of the women you admire?
2. What kinds of problems do mothers solve every day?
3. What is the best contribution a mother can make for her children?
4. How do mothers shape the next generation?
5. How can churches positively impact the health of a home, a family?

Chapter 8

THE ROYAL FAMILY

King David and Absalom

> Children, obey your parents in everything, for this pleases
> the Lord. Fathers, do not embitter your children, or they
> will become discouraged.
>
> —Colossians 3:20–21

The first place a father leads is in his own family. Yet many fathers who lead outside their home struggle to provide leadership for their family, especially for their children. Fathers play an important role in the development of children and the well-being of the family. Sons and daughters need their father's attention and presence in similar ways; they need the same from their mother. Even so, adult children are free to make choices in life that are not consistent with what they learned as children. This scenario can be challenging when the father is also a leader. Both fathers and sons face unique circumstances when a father leads outside the home. The story of King David and his son Absalom brings this truth to the fore.

The nation of Israel was guided by a series of prophets who provided spiritual insight and leadership. However, the people wanted a king they could see and follow. They wanted to be like other nations around them. Their desire to conform to other societies led them

astray from God's plan for them and introduced negative consequences. God granted their request with King Saul and later chose
David as king of Israel. Much can be learned about this Royal Family and the challenges faced by those who seek to lead their family
and to have a godly impact on their lives.

The story begins with David's entry into leadership as a young
man when he was selected and anointed as a future king of Israel.
David was thought to have been an unlikely candidate by his own
brothers and family, but the Lord said to the prophet Samuel, "The
Lord does not look at the things man looks at. Man looks at the outward appearance, but the Lord looks at the heart" (1 Samuel 16:7).
When David arrived at his father's house from the fields where he
was tending sheep, Samuel anointed him, "and from that day on the
Spirit of the Lord came upon David in power" (1 Samuel 16:13).

One of the first things David did on his journey in leadership
was to defeat Goliath, a Philistine warrior from Gath, using a sling
and five smooth stones. Goliath challenged all the men of the army
of Israel to fight on the battlefield. The losers would become the
slaves of the winners. None of the men of Israel's army responded
except David. As Goliath moved toward David on the battlefield,
David ran toward the battle line, took out a smooth stone, loaded it
in his sling, and flung it at Goliath's head, hitting him squarely on
the forehead. Goliath fell face down on the ground, which led to the
defeat of the Philistine army (1 Samuel 17:48–52).

Victory on the battlefield did not necessarily win favor for David
from all quarters. While David's defeat of Goliath and the Philistine army was a victory for David and for the nation of Israel, King
Saul felt jealousy instead. David's popularity grew, and King Saul's
popularity began to diminish. King Saul, who had authorized David
to fight Goliath, became angry and jealous when his men began to
celebrate David's victory. On another occasion, a plot emerged to

have David killed by the Philistines. David succeeded in killing two hundred Philistine soldiers and was awarded King Saul's daughter, Michal, in marriage. When King Saul saw that God's hand was on David, he became more afraid and became David's enemy and planned to have him killed (1 Samuel 18 and 19). Ironically, King Saul's son, Jonathan, became very close friends with David (1 Samuel 20). After many years of tension between King Saul and David, King Saul began to lose battles against the Philistines and lost a final battle at Mount Gilboa. The Philistines captured and killed King Saul's sons Jonathan, Abinadab, and Maki-Shua. King Saul saw the enemy approaching and fell on his own sword and died (1 Samuel 31).

Following the death of King Saul, David was anointed king over Israel and was given promises from the Lord at the beginning of his reign (2 Samuel 7:11–17). The Lord said to David, "Your house and your kingdom will endure forever before me; your throne will be established forever" (7:16). After David's coronation, tension arose between the house of Saul and the house of David (2 Samuel 2:8–31). Yet David was determined to bless the house of Saul. He inquired about any living relatives of King Saul to whom he might show kindness. Ziba, the servant of Saul's household, brought forward the name of Mephibosheth, the son of Jonathan. Mephibosheth was lame in both feet. David summoned him to his palace and gave instructions for Mephibosheth to have land belonging to his grandfather Saul to be restored to him and made provisions for Mephibosheth to eat at David's table all the days of his life. In one sense, for the love of Jonathan, David adopted Mephibosheth, a crippled and vulnerable man, as a son (2 Samuel 9:1–13).

While David was in Hebron, he had six children with different women. Among his children was Amnon, the son of Ahinoam of Jezreel (2 Samuel 3:1–5). Tragedy began to unfold in the Royal Family with the encounter of King David with Bathsheba. He desired her, sent for her, and lay with her. Soon after that encounter, Bathsheba, the wife of Uriah the Hittite, became pregnant with David's child. The king sent Uriah to the front line of battle intending for him to lose his life. Uriah died in a fierce battle, and David took Bathsheba for his wife. Nathan, the prophet, confronted King David about his scheme to marry Bathsheba and have Uriah killed. In due time, Bathsheba gave birth to a son, who died shortly after his birth (2 Samuel 11–12).

Further trouble visited the family of King David when Amnon, one of David's sons, fell in love with Tamar, the beautiful sister of Absalom, another son of David, and consequently, the stepsister of Amnon. Amnon became sad to the point of illness because he could not act on his lust for his half sister. Amnon received advice from his cousin Jonadab on how to seduce Tamar and have sex with her. Tamar fell into the trap and refused to have sex with her half brother Amnon. Amnon refused to listen to the plea of Tamar and raped her. Following the rape, Amnon developed a hatred for Tamar and sent her away. Absalom learned from Tamar about the rape but took no action other than developing a hatred for Amnon because of what he did to Tamar. When King David heard about this, he was furious but took no action in response. Perhaps King David took no action because Amnon was his favored firstborn son.[1]

Two years later, Absalom developed a plot to murder Amnon. He organized his brothers to wait until Amnon was drunk with wine at a party to strike and kill him. Absalom successfully carried out his plan to kill Amnon. After this, Absalom and his brothers rode their mules and fled. Absalom fled while all the other brothers rode to be with King David. When they gathered, they all joined David and mourned Amnon's murder. Absalom stayed in Geshur for three years (2 Samuel 13:1–38). King David loved Amnon and grieved the death of his son and the involvement of his sons in this tragedy.

Absalom's Conspiracy

After several years of living in Geshur, King David sent Joab, one of his servants, to bring Absalom back to Jerusalem. Absalom was a mature, handsome adult. The prophet Samuel said of Absalom, "In all Israel there was not a man so highly praised for his handsome appearance as Absalom. From the top of his head to the sole of his foot there was no blemish in him" (2 Samuel 14:25). Absalom lived in Jerusalem without ever seeing King David in person.

Absalom was not satisfied with living in the shadow of his father, King David, so he began endearing himself to the people who came to visit King David with issues and complaints. He also acquired a chariot and horses with fifty men to run ahead of him. At the end of four years, Absalom requested permission to move to Hebron and the king agreed. There was very little contact or relational engagement between King David and his son Absalom during this time. Absalom declared himself as king over Hebron and amassed a small army of two hundred men all the while developing a conspiracy to usurp his father's throne (2 Samuel 15:1–12). One of King David's servants apprised him of Absalom's plot to overthrow him. The king gathered his family, servants, and army and fled Jerusalem to avoid an attack of Absalom on the Royal Family. David left ten concubines to care for the palace in his absence. Absalom did exactly what David predicted and entered Jerusalem with his army (2 Samuel 15:13–37).

Absalom, under the evil advice of his friend Hushai, began to disgrace his father's palace by having sex with David's concubines in a tent on the roof of the royal palace for all to see. The plan was to provoke his father to attack Jerusalem, but this plan failed (2 Samuel 16:15–23). King David arrived in Mahanaim with his armies, servants, and household. There he organized his army into three groups, appointing commanders of thousands and commanders of hundreds. One third of the army was under the command of Joab, one third under the command of Abishai, Joab's brother, and one third under the command of Ittai, the Gititte (2 Samuel 18:1–3). King David sent out his armies to attack Absalom and his men and gave this word of guidance: "Be gentle with the young man Absalom for my sake" (2 Samuel 18:5). King David's request to treat his son leniently accentuated his love for his son and the hope of a future reconciliation.[2] This command with Absalom as father-king brings together the requirements of the state and the yearnings of a father.[3] The tensions between a father and a son are exacerbated in the case of King David and Absalom.[4]

The Death of Absalom

Absalom's death paints a contrasting picture of family relationships resulting from disobedience and rebellion, as well as adding to the number of children's lives lost in death. King David's army engaged Absalom's army in the forest of Ephraim. Absalom's army suffered heavy losses with as many as twenty thousand men perishing (2 Samuel 18:7). Absalom finally came face-to-face with David's army under the leadership of Joab, the commander. Absalom was riding a mule and began to flee King David's men. As the mule fled under thick branches of an oak tree, Absalom's head was caught in the tree. He was left hanging in midair, while the mule he was riding kept going.

One commentator suggested the phrase "hanging between heaven and earth" is symbolic of Absalom being suspended between life and death, between the sentence of a rebel and the value of a son, between the severity of the king and the yearning of a father.[5] Commander Joab was notified that Absalom was hanging on a tree, so Joab took his javelin and thrust it through Absalom's heart. The rest of Joab's armor-bearers surrounded Absalom, struck, and killed him (2 Samuel 18:14–15).

Absalom could not escape divine judgment. The Lord declared in the Torah that the one who dishonored his father was cursed (Deuteronomy 27:16) and likewise that one who slept with his father's wife was cursed (Deuteronomy 27:20). Absalom had done both.[6] Joab disregarded King David's instructions and took the life of Absalom in the heat of battle. Joab knew better than David himself, who was governed by his parental sensibilities in this situation, that a further pardon of Absalom would only lead to further jeopardizing of the kingdom.[7] The throne of David would not have been secure so long as Absalom lived.[8] The death of Absalom brings to three the number of sons David has lost because of his sins against Bathsheba and her husband Uriah the Hittite.[9]

Joab, the captain of King David's army, sounded a trumpet to signal the battle was over. David's troops stopped pursuing Israel. They took Absalom's body and threw it into a big pit in the forest and piled up a large heap of rocks over him while all the Israelites fled to their homes (2 Samuel 18:16–17). This was the kind of burial offered to an accursed man.[10] It is said by Jewish writers that every passerby was accustomed to throw a stone on the memory of rebellious Absalom and as he threw it to say, "Cursed be the memory of rebellious Absalom; and cursed for ever be all wicked children that rise up in rebellion against their parents."[11] This is the final fruit of Absalom's offense, disobedience to parents who were kind to him, perhaps treating him better than he deserved.[12]

The Grief of a Father

Joab sent Ahimaaz, a messenger, to give David the news of Absalom's death. He entered the king's presence, bowed down before him and said,

"My lord the king, hear the good news! The Lord has delivered you today from all who rose up against you." The king asked the Cushite, "Is the young man Absalom safe?" The Cushite replied,

"May the enemies of my lord the king and all who rise up to harm you be like that young man." The king was shaken. He went up to the room over the gateway and wept. As he went, he said, "O my son Absalom! My son, my son Absalom! If only I had died instead of you—O Absalom, my son, my son!" (2 Samuel 18:31–33)

It seems strange that King David does not ask for details about the death of his son. David offers no reaction at all to the news of the messengers other than a great personal sense of grief and loss. He only wants to know if Absalom is safe.[13] When he heard the news, he cried out Absalom's name three times, indicating the depth of his grief over the loss of his son. The poet-king, who normally was gifted with words at critical times in his life, could only sob at this point.[14] His agony included the loss of his son, the fact that his son died in rebellion without expressing one word of regret, without one request for forgiveness, without one act or word that would be pleasant. David could have said at least one word or phrase that might have softened the blow of death and the fact that his rebellious condition has been passed on to the judgment of God.[15]

King David's grief exposes a difficult predicament for him as king, for his family, and for his subjects. While Absalom was David's son, he was also a traitor. It appears David's grief was much greater than his gratitude to his troops for their victory, and ultimately there was a lack of gratitude to God, who was the real author of his military success.[16] David entered a deep, unrestrained, unguarded grief and perhaps his most and greatest distressed moment.[17] David the father took precedence over David the king, a conflict he lived with during the entire revolt of his son Absalom. He owed this kind of love and devotion to his loyal subjects.[18] It appears that in domestic matters King David was not as accustomed to placing himself under the control of the Divine as he was in the more public business of his life. Consequently, in family matters, he was without the steady influence of submission to the will of God.[19]

David may be grieving more than the death of Absalom. He may also be grieving the death of Bathsheba's son, the rape of Tamar, the murder of Amnon, his loss of the people's trust, and ultimately the knowledge that he is the one to blame for all these losses. The words of Nathan the prophet that "the sword would not depart from his house and that his own family would rise up against him" may have echoed in his mind. David's own sin brought the king to his knees, the kingdom to the ground, and his sons to the grave.[20]

The final refrain from this vignette of grief was King David's statement, "If only I had died instead of you—O Absalom, my son, my son!" (2 Samuel 18:33). In his agony of private grief, King David forgot the public welfare of the nation. One commentator asks, would it have been in the nation's best interest for David to have died instead of Absalom? Imagine what sort of kingdom would have resulted. Imagine the fate and future of the gallant men who fought for David. The condition of God's servants throughout the kingdom would have been damaged. Imagine the influence of a godless monarch such as Absalom in the interests of truth and the cause of God. King David's utterance that he would rather have died instead of Absalom seems to be rash, unadvised words of affection.[21]

The warriors of King David may have felt discouraged. Those who had risked their lives received not a word from their king. They came to realize their king could think of no one except his son, who was now dead. Joab, the captain of David's army approached David and confronted him about issues of humiliating his men, challenged him to think more about the men who fought to save his life, and challenged him to reconsider his love for the son who hated him and his hate for the warriors who love him. Joab warned David that he must immediately go out and encourage his men or risk losing all of them by nightfall (2 Samuel 19:5–7). On that night and on many nights to follow, in the silence of King David's chamber, perhaps for the rest of his life, the thought of that battle and its crowning catastrophe must have haunted David like an ugly dream.[22]

Absalom is a key example of the perils of pride and the personal vanity and extravagance at the expense of his father.[23] The impact of a dysfunctional family is on display in the Royal Family. Rather than a normal functioning family, the consequences of dysfunctional family life impact not only the individuals involved but also the entire nation. The dynamics of the family are at the core of this unfortunate story in the lives of the Royal Family.

Principles of Family Hope

This is a painful story to read. Yet there are several principles we can glean from the Royal Family that may prove helpful to parents today, especially as it relates to the relationship between fathers and sons. There may also be lessons for organizational and ministry leaders who seek to be good parents while managing responsibilities as leaders.

Multiple Wives and Marriages. David appears to have ignored Old Testament teaching on marriage (Genesis 2:24–25). Instead, he had several wives who bore a total of six children. The most prominent marriage was to Bathsheba after the death of Uriah. David was wrong to take advantage of Bathsheba and to order Uriah to the front lines. David's unbridled sexual desire led to tragedy in the lives of those involved.

Parental Discipline and Consequences. When King David learned of the rape of Tamar by Amnon, he took no action, delivered no consequences, and totally ignored the grave injustice on his daughter, the sister of Absalom. Parents must do the challenging work of teaching right behavior and responding with tangible consequences for disobedience. David did neither.

Some commentators suggest Amnon was the favored firstborn son, leading King David to be soft on him and spare him the consequences. Yet withholding consequences for the rape of Tamar only paved the way for Amnon's death at the hands of Absalom. Three years after the rape of Tamar, Absalom planned and carried out the death of Amnon. While David grieved Amnon's death, he executed no consequences on Absalom. David had a parental duty to respond with consequences and had ruling authority as king to respond with consequences and punishment. As difficult as it may feel, parents must step up and provide reasonable consequences for misbehavior and disobedience. Consequences without a personal and genuine relationship with your children breeds contempt. Every effort must be made to develop healthy relationships with children.[24]

Unresolved Conflict. King David never resolved the conflict he must have felt for the disobedience of Absalom. He allowed him to move to Jerusalem, but the biblical record shows they had no contact with each other, no engagement, no relational experiences—none! Hurt feelings, wrongdoing, murder, and misbehavior do not go away by ignoring them. Parents must do the challenging work of reconciling differences and working toward healthy relationships with their adult children, especially when the children have dishonored or disobeyed them. Parents must step up and initiate reconciliation and work on unresolved issues. Unresolved issues will only give rise to a deterioration of the relationship.

Rebellion. Absalom mounted a conspiracy to overthrow his father's reign. This plan turned into an all-out rebellion against his father. Perhaps Absalom lost respect for his father as a father for not acting after Tamar's rape. King David's inaction may have caused further shame on Tamar and her brother Absalom. At some point,

Absalom felt his father was no longer worthy to be king of Israel. The scripture is silent on the motives for Absalom's rebellion. Any hint of rebellious behavior should be taken seriously, and a swift response must be carried out. To ignore rebellion paves the way for a very sad ending and the destruction of parent-child relationships.

Rebellion is a habit born when children are small. Human nature in the smallest of children is normal and natural. Children and youth must be taught to obey, respect, and honor their parents to live out a good life (Ephesians 6:1–3). If our children have come to know Jesus as Savior and Lord, and have been discipled to follow Jesus, remember that they still have a free will like us. There is a difference between control and guidance. Parents should encourage responsibility and freedom as opposed to a lack of guidance and a failure to be properly involved in their children's lives. Each day, they can choose to do what is right or do what is wrong, just like parents. If our children make the wrong choices, it does not mean we were bad parents.

Bad Company. The scripture teaches "bad company corrupts good character" (1 Corinthians 15:33). Parents should pay attention to the friends their children find. Hushai befriended Absalom and encouraged him to shame King David by openly having sex with his concubines to provoke David into battle. When children are young and even into their teen years, parents should monitor the kinds of friends they allow their children to select and spend time with. The wrong friend can undo many years of spiritual training, discipleship, moral teaching, and grounding that parents have provided for children or youth.

Favoritism for Children. King David gave instructions to his army captains to be lenient with Absalom, the traitor who led a rebellion against his father. David's captains and warriors would not have it. They knew leniency would not best serve David's kingdom. We do not do our children favors when we insulate them from consequences or provide a level of favoritism. Ultimately, as in the case of Absalom, we cannot always shield them from inevitable consequences.

Leadership Role Conflict. For parents who are also leaders of ministries, businesses, or organizations where we have influence that impacts our children, every effort must be made to balance and prioritize loyalty to both our children and the organization we serve. Sacrificing the needs of the organization for the benefit of our children is unethical, unfair, and bad practice. The rules, policies, and practices of the organization apply to everyone in the organization. Laws apply to all citizens. Leaders owe it to those who follow them to lead with integrity, honesty, and fairness.

Summary

The story of the Royal Family is difficult to absorb. It is disappointing and tragic, yet it is a story of human families that face challenges. The story shows how our sins can become seeds of family failure, sibling rivalry, sexual misconduct, conflict, murder, and discouragement. Profound lessons can be learned for how to raise children, discipline children, nurture and love them, and lead them into healthy relationships. These are lessons families can learn as they remain intact and share life together. King David was the king the people of Israel wanted, yet the king God ultimately appointed over Israel was born to Joseph and Mary hundreds of years later. They became the Holy Family. What was family life like for Jesus in the Holy Family, and what might we learn from his family life?

Questions for Reflection

1. In what ways can you seek to develop a healthy relationship with your son or daughter?
2. What do sons need most from their fathers?

3. What do daughters need most from the fathers?

4. What is the best way to outline expected behavior and consequences to your children?

5. How can parents help their children choose friends who will affirm the values taught in their home?

Chapter 9

THE HOLY FAMILY

Jesus and His Family

> Go home and love your family.
>
> —Mother Teresa, on being asked
> how to promote world peace

No family is perfect. Not even the family of Jesus. Jesus lived a sinless life, a perfect life as the son of God born of a virgin. Yet he was part of a family of people who were not sinless, not perfect, and not divine in nature. Jesus grew up in a family with parents and siblings who were fully human and not divine. On the other hand, Jesus was fully human and fully divine. You may be wondering what kind of family life Jesus experienced and how his parents and the rest of his family experienced life with him. What can we know about the Holy Family and what lessons might we learn from the family life of Jesus?

We know very little about the Holy Family, yet there is enough biblical evidence to provide some insight into this family. The longest passage of scripture about Jesus is found in Luke 2. We know some about Jesus's visit to the temple as he began to grow, and we know some of his apprenticeship as a carpenter with his earthly father, Joseph. There are a few references in the scriptures to the siblings of

Jesus, and there is some indication that Jesus took responsibility for the care of his parents. Finally, Jesus taught about the family as he gathered disciples during his ministry.

The Birth of Jesus

The story of Jesus's birth begins with his mother, Mary, and his earthly father, Joseph. Mary was engaged to marry Joseph when Gabriel, an angel of the Lord, appeared to Mary to tell her of the birth of her son. Gabriel appeared to Mary and told her she was highly favored by God. Mary was troubled by his words and Gabriel could see her concern, so he told her not to be afraid. Gabriel told Mary, "You will be with child and give birth to a son, and you are to give him the name Jesus. He will be great and will be called the Son of the Most High" (Luke 1:31–32). Gabriel added, "The Lord God will give him the throne of his father David, and he will reign over the house of Jacob forever; his kingdom will never end" (vv. 32–33). Mary asked, "How will this be . . . since I am a virgin?" (v. 34). Gabriel answered that the Holy Spirit of God would come over her in power and the holy one to be born of her would be called the Son of God. Mary's response to this startling announcement was that she was a servant of the Lord, and she said, "May it be to me as you have said" (v. 38).

The Gospel of Luke records the birth of Jesus taking place during a time when the Roman government recorded a census of all its citizens under the reign of Caesar Augustus. This was the first census taken while Quirinius was governor of Syria. Joseph took Mary, who was pregnant and pledged to be married to him, to his hometown of Nazareth. While they were there, the time came for Jesus to be born. Since the cities and towns were crowded with people, there was no room in the inn for them. Joseph found a stable to house his family for the birth of their first son. Once Jesus was born, Mary wrapped him in cloths and placed him in a manger. The practice of wrapping a child in swaddling cloths was a mark of maternal care common to any ancient Palestinian mother's care of her newborn.[1]

On the outskirts of Bethlehem, there were shepherds tending to their sheep in the fields. They could not have imagined anything out of the ordinary and certainly not an announcement about a child being born to a young couple. "An angel of the Lord appeared to them, . . . and they were terrified. But the angel said to them, 'Do not be afraid. I bring you good news of great joy that will be for all the people. Today in the town of David a savior has been born to you; he is Christ the Lord. This will be a sign to you: You will find a baby wrapped in cloths and lying in a manger'" (2:9–12). The birthday announcement of Jesus not only signaled good news for the nation of Israel but also good news to a young couple, and the start of a family. The arrival of Jesus at his birth was marked by unprecedented celebration among the angels of God. Many angels appeared with Gabriel and began to worship and praise God saying, "Glory to God in the highest, and on earth peace to men on whom his favor rests" (v. 14). After this burst of praise, the angels left and went back to heaven. The shepherds turned to one another and said, "Let's go to Bethlehem and see this thing that has happened, which the Lord has told us about" (v. 15). The shepherds found the Holy Family through a supernatural announcement. They found Mary and Joseph and their baby lying in a manger. After they saw Jesus, they spread the word about him, and all who heard it were amazed. Mary treasured all these things in her heart. The shepherds went on their way responding like the angels, glorifying and praising God.

The arrival of the wise men who traveled from the East made the birth of Jesus an international event. In response to Herod's intentions to eliminate all newborns, Joseph led Mary and Jesus to Egypt as refugees.

Jesus as a Child and Young Man

It was customary at that time to circumcise a son and declare his official name eight days after he was born. Joseph and Mary took Jesus to Jerusalem for this ceremony. The Mosaic law required every firstborn to be consecrated to the Lord along with a sacrificial offering of two doves or two young pigeons (vv. 21–24). Offering two doves or two young pigeons would have been a customary offering from poor and middle-class families.[2]

Once Joseph and Mary completed all the requirements of the Law of Moses, they returned to Galilee where they made their home in Nazareth. Jesus grew up in a family that meticulously observed the Law of Moses. From birth he was brought up in the moral and ritual life of Judaism. Home, temple, and synagogue formed him, including the ceremony of bar mitzvah, meaning "son of the law," at age twelve.[3] The Gospel of Luke provides a glimpse of Jesus as a child saying, "The child grew and became strong; he was filled with wisdom, and the grace of God was upon him" (v. 40).

The only other glimpse of the early childhood of Jesus is when he was twelve years old. As a preteen, Jesus went with his parents to Jerusalem for the Feast of the Passover, a one-way trip of approximately eighty miles.[4] This annual trip to celebrate the Passover Festival was a popular family affair for the average Jewish family and was designed to commemorate Israel's communal identity as God's firstborn son as depicted in Exodus 4:22.[5]

At the age of twelve, Jesus would be, in terms of the culture of the day, beginning to transition from childhood to adulthood.[6] All Jewish men and boys were expected to "appear before the Lord," at the great festivals, and Mary and Joseph showed themselves to be God-fearing and obedient citizens by taking their son to Jerusalem when he reached age twelve after the custom of the feast, as well as other feasts required by the Mosaic Law. As far as we know, this is the first visit to the temple since his infancy.[7] After the Feast was over, his parents returned home, but Jesus stayed behind in Jerusalem. The words used to describe Jesus staying behind convey the idea of persistence and perseverance and are used of remaining after others have gone. The attraction of divine things held him fast, despite the departure of his parents. This would be his first experience of the temple services and especially of the slaying of the Paschal lamb.[8]

His parents were unaware of Jesus's absence. They were under the impression that Jesus was in the company of family and friends returning to Nazareth and traveled a day's journey before they realized he was not with them. Joseph and Mary began to look for Jesus among the group traveling together but could not find him. They returned to Jerusalem to look for him. After three days of searching, they found Jesus in the temple courts, sitting among the teachers of the law, listening and engaging them with questions. Everyone who heard Jesus was amazed at his understanding and answers. Luke is presenting Jesus as a child of remarkable intellect and insight.[9] The home-schooling of Jesus in Nazareth proved formative not only for his maturing as a human but also as a divine agent during this three-day seminar with temple scholars in Jerusalem.[10] Jesus also had the opportunity to learn about the Jewish religion and customs at his local synagogue.

When Joseph and Mary saw Jesus, they were astonished. Mary asked Jesus, "Why have you treated us like this? Your father and I have been anxiously searching for you" (v. 48). Three days of anxiety may have contributed to Mary's intense rebuke of Jesus.[11] One author noted the word used to describe the anxiety of Jesus's parents is *odynomenoi*, meaning deep mental anguish and pain.[12] Another author suggested Mary and Joseph may have experienced anger and shame at having lost Jesus and for having been put in this predicament.[13] Another suggested that Mary and Joseph may have been astonished, shocked, or dumbfounded at their son's behavior. Independence, in their time, represented insolence rather than a proactive initiative admired by Westerners today.[14]

Mary engaged Jesus on multiple levels. "*Intellectually*, asking him for a rational explanation; *actively*, reporting her extended search for Jesus; and *emotionally*, expressing her 'great anxiety.'"[15] At the same time, Mary and Joseph may not have fully realized that since Jesus was the Messiah, there was no reason to be anxious about his welfare.[16] Jesus answered and said, "Why were you searching for me? . . . Didn't you know I had to be in my father's house?" (v. 49). Jesus makes a sharp turn in his redefinition of the term *father* that may have led to his parents to reflect further on what he meant.[17] One author noted that, to us, after many centuries of Christian teaching and saying the Lord's prayer, the Fatherhood of God has become "so axiomatic that we scarcely think about it." But to Mary and Joseph, and even to the rabbis and doctors of the law, Jesus's words must have sounded strange. While there are references to God as Father of the Jewish people in the Old Testament, the idea of a personal and paternal relationship between God and the soul is practically unknown at this point in time.[18] Jesus may also have been genuinely surprised and somewhat grieved at the distress he caused his parents.[19]

His parents did not understand what Jesus meant with those questions. The fact that Luke records Mary's lack of understanding is designed to make the point to his readers of the difficulty of understanding who Jesus is or was.[20] They were unable to see his identity as the Son of God. One author questioned how they could not have understood this by asking, "Did they not know that Jesus was conceived of the Holy Spirit? Did Mary forget Elizabeth's words that her unborn child was the Lord? What about the adoration of the shepherd's at Jesus's birth?" Evidently, all these things became vague memories over the course of time. The daily contact with the human Jesus had an effect of forgetting the divine statements made about him.[21] This episode in the life of Jesus is the first indication that he is aware of his special mission and hints at conflicts between that mission and family expectations.[22] Jesus demonstrated a submissive attitude toward his parents as he rejoined them for the journey back home.[23] Once again, Mary treasured all those experiences in her heart.

Jesus continued to grow in wisdom and stature, and in favor with God and men (Luke vv. 41–52). Quite literally, Jesus grew like other children. He gained weight and stature. He became strong and full of wisdom.[24] This experience and his place in the family, his loyalty and devotion to his parents, and his calling to fulfill his divine mission and obedience to God provided Joseph and Mary much to consider over the following nineteen years of his life prior to his ministry.[25] Jesus spent a total of thirty years with this family and in family life before his three-year ministry. Today, most seminary students spend three years in preparation for a thirty-year ministry.

The Siblings of Jesus

Joseph and Mary continued to grow their family with several children. We know about his siblings from an account of Jesus teaching in the synagogue on the Sabbath in his hometown of Nazareth, accompanied by his disciples. Many who heard him were amazed. Some of his listeners began to ask, "Where did this man get these things? . . . What's this wisdom that has been given him, that he even does miracles! Isn't this the carpenter? Isn't this Mary's son and the brother of James, Joseph, Judas and Simon? Aren't his sisters here with us?" Some of the crowd took offense at Jesus's teaching (Mark 6:1–6).

From this passage, it is evident that Jesus had four brothers and at least two sisters, maybe more. Jesus's mother and brothers were said to have waited to speak to Jesus as he was addressing a crowd (Matthew 12:46–47, Mark 3:31, and Luke 8:19). Jesus also traveled with his mother and brothers, as well as his disciples, to Capernaum (John 2:12). After the death and resurrection of Jesus, his mother, Mary, and the brothers of Jesus joined with the disciples of Jesus to pray (Acts 1:14).

The apostle Paul asked Jesus about who was eligible to marry a believing wife. Paul referenced the apostles and the brothers of Jesus, as the Lord's brothers, who married (1 Corinthians 9:5). James, one of the half-brothers of Jesus is the author of the Epistle of James in the New Testament, and an apostle of Jesus. He described himself as a servant of God and of the Lord Jesus Christ (James 1:1). Paul identified James as the Lord's brother in his letter to the Christian churches in the region of Galatia (Galatians 1:19).

While it is clear that Jesus had siblings, the Bible does not provide much record or insight as to their relationships throughout their adolescence or even about their lives as adults. We know that the family of Jesus were often together with their mother, Mary, when engaging Jesus. We know that Jesus grew up in a rather large family and that he helped his earthly father, Joseph, who was a carpenter. We also know Jesus took on the role as head of the family after Joseph died and continued to provide for his family, including his mother and younger siblings.[26]

Jesus's Teaching About Family

Jesus taught that children were to be valued. He demonstrated care for the widow as well. He also knew and taught that loyalty to family had limitations for those who chose to be his disciples. People were bringing children to Jesus so he might lay hands on them and bless them, but his disciples, seeking to protect Jesus, rebuked those who brought them. When Jesus saw what was happening, he said, "Let the little children come to me, and do not hinder them, for the kingdom of God belongs to such as these." Jesus placed his hands on the children to bless them and then went on from there (Matthew 19:13–15; Mark 10:14; and Luke 18:15–17). Jesus highlighted the simple faith of children and said, "Anyone who will not receive the kingdom of God like a little child will never enter it." He then took children into his arms and blessed them (Mark 10:15–16).

Jesus also had compassion for senior adults. When Jesus was on the cross his mother, his mother's sister, Mary the wife of Clopas, and Mary Magdalene stood nearby. John, the beloved disciple, also stood near Mary, the mother of Jesus. Jesus saw his mother standing there with John and said to his mother, " 'Dear woman, here is your son' and to the disciple, 'Here is your mother.' From that time on, this disciple took her into his home" (John 19:25–27). The Catholic Church has historical documentation that John, the apostle, carried out much of his work in Ephesus and brought Mary, the mother of Jesus, with him. A church dedicated to the memory of Mary, the mother of Jesus, still stands in Ephesus, Turkey, today. This is the place where Mary would have lived and died.

While Jesus appeared to value families and the care of children and seniors, especially his mother, he also taught that there were limitations to family ties for people who agreed to be his disciple. Jesus came to call men and women to allegiance to him as disciples over and above one's loyalty to his or her own family. Jesus said, "Anyone who loves his father or mother more than me is not worthy of me; . . . and anyone who does not take his cross and follow me is not worthy of me" (Matthew 10:37–38). He also said, "If anyone comes to me and does not hate father and mother, his wife and children, his brothers and sisters—yes, even his own life—he cannot be my disciple" (Luke 14:26). What Jesus refers to here is not literal hate but a matter of priority. For the disciple, Jesus must be his or her priority, even over one's life. In fact, Jesus promised a greater return of blessing in the age to come for those willing to leave home, brothers, sisters, mother, father, children, or fields to follow him (Mark 10:29–31). Jesus broadened the definition of *family* as anyone who does the will of God, therefore elevating followers of Jesus into the realm of the most intimate relationships of family (Mark 3:31–35).

The story of the Holy Family provides limited insight into the family of Jesus. Yet there is ample evidence of a healthy family experience and environment into which Jesus was born, grew, and matured. Ample teaching is also available from Jesus's family about the nature of human families related to God as our heavenly father in matters of faith, obedience, and loyalty.

Principles of Family Hope

Through the story of the Holy Family, we can learn lessons about how to relate to the government, the sanctity of life, the spiritual formation of families, the calling to one's family and to faith, how to bless children, how to become part of the family of faith, and how to care for our parents.

Families and the Government. All human families are subject to human authorities and local governments. At the time of Jesus's birth, his family was responding to a national census underway that caused them to return to their hometown of Bethlehem. Families of faith are also expected to respond to government regulations and local laws in responsible ways. Parents are wise to teach their children to have a healthy respect for law and order as they plan and live out their lives according to God's will on earth.

Sanctity of Life. Mary nurtured her firstborn son with care, love, and protection as common by mothers throughout the ages. Mothers naturally are inclined to nurture and care for their children. Joseph was also concerned about preserving the life of his son and led the Holy Family to flee to Egypt for safety reasons. Fathers are naturally concerned about providing food, shelter, and safety for their families. Children are a gift from God and deserve nurture, care, bonding, safety, security, and nourishment to grow and develop into mature human beings. Mary and Joseph must have learned these lessons from their families of origin.

Spiritual Formation of Families. Mary and Joseph oriented Jesus to their faith and practice of Jewish religious ritual and customs. They meticulously followed the Law of Moses. It is the primary duty and responsibility to take on the spiritual formation of their children. Fathers have the responsibility to ensure children are educated and oriented in their religious tradition. Parents are the primary evangelists and disciple-makers of their children and are responsible to teach them everything Jesus commanded. All religious practices provided by religious leaders, religious rituals, or programs are supplemental to foundational spiritual formation in the home. Spiritual formation habits of prayer, Bible reading, Bible teaching, and worship should be experienced at home and supplemented by the local church.

Calling to Family and Faith. Parents are responsible to orient their children to a sense of belonging in their family. Children should be taught values like loyalty, integrity, and honesty. However, loyalty and devotion should not be taught as superior to one's devotion to God and his call on a person's life. Children should be taught to listen to the voices of their father and mother. They should be taught the meaning of obedience and compliance. Once these lessons are learned from earthly fathers and mothers, they will already be in the habit of responding in obedience and faith when the heavenly voice calls them.

Blessing Children. Children are to be cherished and blessed at every opportunity. This was the habit of Jesus. He acknowledged, made time for, made space for, nurtured, and encouraged children. Jesus taught that we must become like children to inherit the kingdom of heaven. He taught us we must have childlike faith. Children should be nurtured, encouraged, and blessed as key members of the family, the community, and the family of faith rather than seen as an inconvenience. However, parents should not make children the center of life, place their children on a pedestal, or spoil them.

The Family of God. All children should be taught about the difference between their human family and the family of faith. The simple plan of salvation should be modeled and then taught to children with an opportunity given to them to respond to faith at the earliest age possible. Children should be taught to honor and obey their parents in addition to listening to and responding to the voice of God as they grow into teens and adults.

Care for Parents and Senior Adults. Jesus was devoted to his mother even at the point of his death. Parents are to be honored and revered throughout their lives. The welfare of parents is the responsibility of their children, regardless of the age of their adult children. Jesus assumed the responsibility for the care of his mother as a young adult. The primary responsibility for the care of parents belongs to their children.

Summary

The story of the Holy Family is full of humanity and divinity. While the family of Jesus was not perfect, he was. The dynamics of the Holy Family with a mixture of humanity and divinity teaches us many lessons about healthy families as well as their limitations in the realm of faith. The roles and responsibilities of parents are clear in this story as modeled by Mary and Joseph. The pattern of family and faith set forth in the family of Jesus reverberates through-out human history, even in the twenty-first century. The message of Jesus transforms families, even the most unlikely families. What does family life look like for a Roman soldier who comes to faith? How is that family impacted and transformed? The next chapter answers these questions.

Questions for Reflection

1. How do families nurture a proper understanding and perspective on the government and governing authorities?
2. What is your plan to spiritually form the children in your family, besides taking them to church?
3. In what ways does your family nurture, value, and celebrate children?
4. How is faith in Jesus Christ developed and talked about in your family?
5. What is your plan for caring for your aging parents in times of health and in times of need?

Chapter 10

THE TRANSFORMED FAMILY

The Philippian Jailer

It is easier to build strong children than to repair broken men.

—Frederick Douglass

The presence of a father in a family is essential for the well-being of children and the economic stability, safety, and security of a family. But mere presence does not always translate into a positive, healthy environment for those who live in the household. One might argue that a family with a toxic, cruel, abusive, and detached father may do more harm in a home than one who is absent. Fathers must be not only present but also invested, engaged, interested, resourceful, and in tune with the needs of their wives and children. If possible, he will be transformed by the power of Jesus and shaped into his character. You may have met a broken father, but have you met a transformed father?

Frederick Douglass is right. Repairing a broken man takes lots of energy and effort, perhaps much more than raising strong children. Yet repairing a broken man is not impossible with the transforming power of the gospel.

The Context

Dr. Luke chronicled the actions, or the acts, of the first-century church in the Acts of the Apostles. In chapter 16, the apostle Paul is the central figure in this part of the story of the early church. He selected a young man named Timothy, the son of a Greek man and a Jewish woman, who was a believer in Jesus. Timothy was well spoken of by the believers in the cities of Lystra and Iconium, in modern-day Turkey.

Timothy joined Paul and Silas as they passed through these cities delivering decrees decided upon by the apostles to strengthen and encourage the churches established there. They listened to and were led by the Holy Spirit through places like Phrygia, Galatia, Mysia, Bithynia and Troas, also in modern-day Turkey. While in Troas, Paul received a vision in the night of a man in Macedonia who said, "Come over to Macedonia and help us." Paul, Silas, and Timothy immediately went to Macedonia to preach. They traveled by sea from Troas to Samothrace, Neapolis, and then to Philippi, the leading city of the district of Macedonia, a Roman colony in modern day Greece (Acts 16:1–12).

Once in Philippi, Paul's team met a woman named Lydia, from the city of Thyatira, who was a business leader marketing fabric. She was also a worshipper of God with a sensitivity to spiritual matters. Luke says the Lord opened her heart to respond to the good news spoken by Paul. She and her family responded in faith to the message Paul preached and were baptized. She invited them into her home to stay with her family.

The next day they were headed to the place of prayer and met a slave girl possessed by a spirit of divination, who generated a large amount of revenue for her masters by fortune telling. She followed Paul and his team and cried out, saying, "'These men are servants of the Most High God, who are telling you the way to be saved.' She kept this up for many days. Finally Paul became so troubled that he turned around and said to the spirit, 'In the name of Jesus Christ I command you to come out of her!' At that moment, the spirit left her" (vv. 17–18).

When the owners of the slave girl realized that their revenue stream was disrupted,

> they seized Paul and Silas and dragged them into the marketplace to face the authorities. They brought them before the magistrates and said, 'These men are Jews, and are throwing our city into an uproar by advocating customs unlawful for us Romans to accept or practice.' The crowd joined in the attack against Paul and Silas, and the magistrates ordered them to be stripped and beaten. After they had been severely flogged, they were thrown into prison, and the jailer was commanded to guard them carefully. Upon receiving such orders, he put them in the inner cell and fastened their feet in stocks. (Acts 16:19–24)

The Philippian Jailer

Dr. Thom Wolf coined the phrase, "Roman soldiers never die, they simply retire at Philippi."[1] Wolf made the case that a Roman soldier is not someone you would want to meet in a dark alley. A jailer was typically a Roman soldier who had proven his loyalty to the Roman government through a life of service. Roman soldiers were professional warriors highly skilled in the art of war. They were experienced in battle and had the ability to quickly annihilate their opponents. Details of the Roman skills of hand-to-hand combat and dismemberment of human bodies would shock most of us even today. These jailers were decorated warriors awarded with the position of jailer as a retirement job with benefits.[2] The type of man tasked with the responsibility of guarding Paul and Silas was a seasoned veteran, a no-nonsense type of rough and tough man. He was provided a private residence as a benefit of the job. His family lived with him and were well aware of the effect that military service, feats, and conquests had on him over the years. What comes next is a dramatic story of transformation of this man.

Midnight Madness

Luke, the physician recording this story, reported that about midnight following the day of Paul and Silas's arrest, these men were praying and singing hymns to God with an audience of other prisoners. The two believers mixed both petition and praise as they sat in chains.[3] Suddenly a violent earthquake shook the foundations of the prison. All the prison doors flew open and the chains of all the prisoners came loose. "If the prison was excavated from rocks in the hillside, as was often the case, the earthquake would easily have slipped the bars of the doors loose and the chains would have fallen out of the walls."[4]

The jailer would have been asleep at the top of the prison and his silhouette visible against the moonlight since the lights were out. The jailer woke up, and when he saw the doors of the prison open, he drew his sword and was about to kill himself because he thought the prisoners had escaped. Taking his own life would have been the only honorable thing a jailer could do since he was personally responsible for the prisoners with his own life.[5] It was understood that a jailer's failure to contain his prisoners would come at a high cost.

"But Paul shouted, 'Don't harm yourself! We are all here!' The jailer called for lights, rushed in and fell trembling before Paul and Silas. He then brought them out and asked, 'Sirs, what must I do to be saved?' They replied, 'Believe in the Lord Jesus, and you will be saved—you and your household'" (Acts 16:25–31). Paul was not saying the jailer's faith would result in the salvation of the whole family. Rather, Paul was offering the same message of salvation to all the jailer's family.[6]

132

At some point in the evening, the jailer and the prisoners may have talked about why Paul and Silas were in stocks. The other prisoners would have most likely asked them what they had done to be put in jail. They may have asked them why they were judged so harshly and unfairly. They may have commented on the way they were falsely accused with no trial. They may have wondered how prisoners in that condition would resort to prayer and singing hymns. Paul and Silas no doubt also talked about faith in Jesus and all they had experienced that day with the slave girl. These conversations, the prayers of Paul and Silas, and their songs of praise may have been the last words and music they heard before they all drifted into sleep and before the earthquake shook the prison and woke them up.

The jailer's first thought had been that all was lost, and all prisoners had escaped, but he was wrong. The first action he took was to draw his sword to take his life. The first voice he heard was Paul's saying, "Wait! Don't harm yourself. All is not lost. All are not gone. We are here." The first question the jailer asked Paul and Silas was "What do I have to do to be saved?" The jailer may have heard of Jesus as the way of salvation from the slave girl who revealed the message Paul and Silas were sharing.[7]

Bringing It Home

The next vignette is a scene in the jailer's house where Paul and Silas can provide a fuller explanation of the good news to the jailer and his family.[8] It is likely the jailer's home was built on top of the prison since the jailer "brought them up" there.[9] The jailer brought Paul and Silas into his home, where Paul spoke the message of salvation and faith in Jesus to the jailer and all the others in his household. Since the earthquake occurred at midnight, by the time the jailer is in his home, it must be the early hours of the morning. His family is awake, trying to figure out what just happened. The jailer brought prisoners into the courtyard of his house, but they were not chained. The jailer's wife and those living in his home, perhaps adult children and their children or his guests, were disoriented. We don't know what the jailer said to explain the presence of prisoners in their home, but we do know that Paul and Silas had an audience and an introduction to share the gospel with the jailer, his family, and their guests, all who were in the household. What happens next can only be explained by a transformed heart, a spirit of gratitude, and a radical transformation of the mind.

From Making Wounds to Washing Wounds

What happens when a broken, hardened military officer and veteran is confronted by the message of redemption, salvation, forgiveness of sin, and the potential of a new life? What would that look like in the first century? How are families impacted by a spiritually transformed father? What kind of change can we expect from a father who has been transformed by the message of Jesus? Does the gospel message still have the power to reshape fathers and families in the twenty-first century?

By this time, it must have been after one a.m. or later. The jailer took Paul and Silas, perhaps to the courtyard where the fountain flowed, and washed their wounds. His wife may have brought out linens to dip into the fountain, yet it was the jailer who washed the wounds of Paul and Silas (16:33). Recall that this seasoned veteran was experienced in making wounds on other people. But now he is washing wounds. His family witnessed the transformation of this father. They may have never seen him wash the wounds of anyone, but now he is washing the wounds of prisoners. Then after the wound-washing is finished, the jailer and all his family were baptized (v. 33).

"As elsewhere in Acts, baptism of the household reflects a culture in which the head (Cornelius, Lydia, the jailer) decides on behalf of all, and that all includes not only the immediate family but the extended family, as well as slaves and their families."[10] Another author added that the New Testament takes the unity of family seriously, and when salvation is offered to the head of the household, it is as a matter of course made available to the rest of the family group including servants.[11] Now it's time to celebrate.

Party Time!

After the baptism to publicly identify as followers of Jesus Christ, the jailer brought Paul and Silas back to his home to celebrate his new faith. It is now possibly two or three a.m., and it is time for a party. The jailer set a meal before Paul and Silas as his guests of honor. The words in Greek for this behavior are *paretheken trapezan*, meaning "he set a table, prepared a meal."[12] Again, has his family ever seen anything like this? Have they witnessed any level of gratitude or hospitality from their decorated warrior-veteran-jailer father? Why did the jailer do these things in front of his family and guests? He was "filled with joy because he had come to believe in God—he and his whole family" (v. 34). The sharing of a meal denoted a sense of community and extended the motif of hospitality between believing Jews and Gentiles.[13] The good news of Jesus creates a new community among believers. The family believed in Jesus from the words spoken to them by Paul. However, they were also likely moved by the change of heart, the transformation of the life of their father in their presence. The message was powerful and so was the impact on their father. They were persuaded and convinced that this was the way to live from that point on as publicly identified with Jesus of Nazareth.

The Next Day

The jailer told Paul and Silas the magistrates had ordered them to be freed. Paul and Silas were to go in peace. But Paul said to the officers, "They beat us publicly without a trial, even though we are Roman citizens, and threw us into prison. And now do they want to get rid of us quietly? No! Let them come themselves and escort us out" (v. 37). This was an effort to publicly acknowledge that Paul and Silas had been wronged and mistreated.[14] "The officers reported this to the magistrates, and when they heard that Paul and Silas were Roman citizens, they were alarmed. They came to appease them and escorted them from the prison, requesting them to leave the city. After Paul and Silas came out of the prison, they went to Lydia's house, where they met with the brothers and encouraged them. Then they left" (vv. 38–40). After undergoing brutal and unfair treatment, Paul and Silas insisted on being treated according to their rights as citizens while maintaining their priority and focus on the mission of sharing the gospel with as many as possible in Philippi.

The story of the Philippian jailer demonstrates the power of the gospel to change a man, a warrior, and a father. It provides a glimpse of first-century life, the early proclamation of the gospel led by the Holy Spirit, and its effect on prisoners, guards, fathers, families, slaves, and government officials. The impact of the gospel on this one man transformed not only him but also his family and his entire household.

Principles of Family Hope

Several principles arise from the story of the Philippian jailer related to the power of the gospel for parents and children, the potential of good news in times of crises, the power of living out our faith in the presence of our families, and basic citizenship rights afforded to parents and children.

Gospel Power for Families. The power of the gospel can change a man at any age. It can change a family at any stage of its existence. The gospel requires proclamation, announcement, and explanation for faith to arise. Faith comes by hearing. Heads of households who come to faith have influence on the availability of the gospel message to everyone in the household. While this was particularly true in the first century, it is also true today. The gospel that comes to parents should also flow through them to the rest of their household.

Good News in Crises. We can never know the crises people face. A crisis of vocation, economics, or relationship tends to create an openness to good news and to solutions for life. Fathers and mothers often bear many burdens and are looking for hope of a better life. If we listen and if we are attentive to the needs of struggling parents, we will hear their concerns and deepest needs and know how to respond with a ready answer for the reason of our hope in Christ.

Transformed Living. Nothing compares to the visible demonstration of a transformed father or mother. Parents who imitate the example and way of Jesus in the presence of their children will embed the gospel message in ways far superior to any pulpit available to them. The strongest proclamation of the gospel comes through the demonstration of living impacted by the presence of Jesus in a parent's life. Your children are constantly watching and observing the faith lived in your life. Your actions will always speak louder than your words.

Family Rights. At its best, citizenship of parents and families in their country comes with inalienable rights and responsibilities. Faith in Jesus does not cancel those rights. However, care should be taken to place priority of sharing the gospel and the mission entrusted to us over our rights as citizens. When possible, families should not shrink back from insisting on basic rights afforded to them by the government.

Summary

Families form the foundation of villages, communities, cities, counties, states, and nations. Parents lead families, nurture children, provide and protect them, and create a healthy environment in which to grow and develop. Fathers are pivotal in the success of a family in that they provide and protect their families with love and sacrifice. Mothers raise children with the help of their husbands and provide for the care and nurture of their families. A father that is present and available and leads his family spiritually has the potential of shaping the next generation of leaders for the community. A transformed father will have incredible influence in building faith-oriented children who are contributors to society wherever they go, yet I realize that parental rights are not recognized or respected in some nations in the global village. The next chapter will describe what a faith-flourishing family looks like.

Questions for Reflection

1. How is the gospel message of faith in Jesus Christ for salvation, forgiveness, and redemption best shared in the context of your family?
2. What kinds of crises do families face that call for the hope of the gospel message?
3. In what ways can parents demonstrate their faith to their children in everyday moments of life?
4. What types of conversations lend themselves to gospel awareness within the context of family life?
5. What basic rights are afforded to families in our society today?

Chapter 11

THE FLOURISHING FAMILY

Lois, Eunice, and Timothy

Children's children are a crown to the aged,
and parents are the pride of their children.

—Proverbs 17:6

Families that flourish grow and develop in healthy and vigorous ways. Children in families that flourish have parents who know their roles and responsibilities to raise and nurture the next generation. These children have a sense of confidence, belonging, and purpose. The purpose of flourishing families is to fulfill their talents and potential for the greater good of their community. Flourishing families have all the resources they need to thrive, including a spiritual faith foundation.

Sociologist Carle Zimmerman, founding director of the Sociology Department at Harvard University, published works on the family as a foundational unit for civilizations. In his book, *Family and Civilization*, Zimmerman documents three family types in the first century: trustee families, domestic families, and atomistic families. Trustee families had maximum power and authority over the individual and family units; domestic families provided a middle ground of influence; and atomistic families were weak and did not hold much power or influence emphasizing individualism and freeing the individual from family bonds.

Zimmerman notes that the Roman government sought to destabilize trustee families who carried too much power and authority over societies in that era. The Roman state attempted to empower and favor the domestic family type, which is common throughout the modern world. Atomistic families became the predominant family style highlighting individualism after the fifth century BC in Greek culture and after the reign of Augustus in Rome (27 BCE through AD 14). This family type became popular in the eighteenth and nineteenth century of our day.[1] From the middle of the fifth century BC to the Roman occupation through the middle of the second century, classic Greek societies experienced the rise and decay of atomistic families.[2] It appears that the rise of the atomistic family contributed to the fall of Roman civilization. Zimmerman concludes the following:

> In general, the most important contribution of the family to great civilizations has been made by the domestic unit. . . . The trustee family never produced anything greater than the heroic epic. It belongs to primitive formative periods of civilization. . . . The atomistic family, when it attains complete dominance, is the accompaniment of dying cultures. The creative periods in civilization have been based upon the domestic type. The end of a creative period is always one in which the domestic type is submerged into the atomistic. This seems due to the fact that the domestic family affords a comparatively stable social structure and yet frees the individual from family influence to perform the creative work necessary for a great civilization.[3]

Given Zimmerman's conclusions, what does the future hold for the family? Zimmerman says, "that the family of the immediate future will move further toward atomism seems highly probable. Except for the Christian Church—which at present is not popular among the directive forces of Western society—no agency or group of persons seems fundamentally interested in doing anything other than facilitating this increasing atomism."[4] What marks the Christian Church family that causes the domestic type of family unit to flourish? Is this type of family a positive influence for the success of civilizations now and in the future? What is it about the Christian family that distinguishes itself from other family types, and how do these families contribute to the flourishing of communities, societies, and civilizations? The exploration of one first-century family may provide answers.

Timothy: First-Century Community Leader, Pastor, Author

Timothy, a disciple and mentee of the apostle Paul, served as a community leader and pastor. He also coauthored the letter to the Christians at Thessalonica. In chapter 10 of this book, I mentioned how Paul recruited Timothy to serve with him as a missionary colleague. Timothy became a disciple of Jesus in the town of Lystra, where the good news reached. His father was Greek, and his mother was a Jewish follower of Jesus. Timothy was circumcised because he was a Greek convert and joined Paul in his second missionary journey (Acts 16:1–5).

Later in their ministry, Paul sent Timothy to resolve problems at the church in Corinth. In a letter to the Corinthian church, Paul states, "For this reason I am sending to you Timothy, my son whom I love, who is faithful in the Lord. He will remind you of my way of life in Christ Jesus, which agrees with what I teach everywhere in every church" (1 Corinthians 4:17). Paul mentored Timothy to serve as a church leader and pastor.

Timothy spent time with Paul and earned the reputation of being faithful in his relationship with the Lord. He also learned Paul's way of living in Christ, the bedrock of Paul's teaching everywhere he encountered a local body of believers formed into a church, a set-apart faith community. Paul refers to this "way of living in Christ" that he taught in a letter to Timothy. He wrote, "What you heard from me, keep as the pattern of sound teaching, with faith and love in Christ Jesus. Guard the good deposit that was entrusted to you— guard it with the help of the Holy Spirit who lives in us" (2 Timothy 1:13–14). Thom Wolf researched the concept of a first-century pattern of ethical education for leadership from this reference to the "pattern of sound teaching."[5]

Paul wrote the Christians in Corinth and urged them to receive and support Timothy during his visit. He wrote, "If Timothy comes, see to it that he has nothing to fear while he is with you, for he is carrying on the work of the Lord, just as I am. No one, then, should refuse to accept him. Send him on his way in peace so that he may return to me. I am expecting him along with the brothers" (1 Corinthians 16:10–11). It is apparent Paul trusted Timothy and lent him the credibility of his name, his reputation, and his influence. Paul sent Timothy in his place to do the work of the Lord.

Timothy became the leader at the Christian church at Ephesus. Paul instructed Timothy to go to Ephesus and teach the church to avoid false teaching and doctrines and to avoid devotion to myths and endless genealogies that promote controversy rather than God's work done by faith (1 Timothy 1:3–4). Paul engaged Timothy in producing letters to the church at Thessalonica and to Philemon (1 Thessalonians 1:1; 2 Thessalonians 1:1; and Philemon 1:1). Paul mentored Timothy as a developer of leaders. He encouraged Timothy to entrust the pattern of teaching to reliable men who will also be qualified to teach others. He provided examples of leadership development experiences to describe qualities in future leaders like that of a soldier, an athlete, and a farmer-businessman. He reminded Timothy that the Lord would provide him with insight into leadership development (2 Timothy 2:1–7). Paul discipled Timothy, and he taught him how to disciple others and raise up leadership for the first-century faith communities that Paul, Silas, and Timothy began. Where did this young man named Timothy come from? What kind of family produces this kind of leader?

Faith Formation in Timothy

The apostle Paul speaks of Timothy as his spiritually adopted son in the Lord.[6] Timothy's biological father was not a believer and, therefore, not influential in the development of Timothy's faith.[7] One author agreed that Timothy's father was either not alive or not involved in Timothy's spiritual formation.[8]

Paul remembered Timothy in his prayers and pointed to Timothy's sincere faith. This faith in Jesus Christ began in Timothy's grandmother Lois and in his mother, Eunice. The mention of Lois and Eunice, Jewish women with Greek names, only occurs here in the entire New Testament.[9] Paul was convinced this same faith in Christ was resident in Timothy. Paul used the verb *lives* when describing how the faith of Timothy's grandmother and mother existed in him. This word means "to be at home," indicating the depth and extent to which their faith had become an integral part of their lives.[10]

The family is the transmitter of faith. In Judaism, the family was and is the primary locus for passing on the tradition of faith from generation to generation.[11] What is striking in this second letter to Timothy is that grandmothers, mothers, and sons have a lot to do with one another.[12] It is clear that women and men form an integral part of discipling spiritual leaders for the church.[13] The

Hebrew Scripture Timothy's mother and grandmother taught him during his childhood contributed to his spiritual development and maturity.[14] The role of faith development in the family cannot be overemphasized as well as the telling and retelling of faith stories and the nurturing of memories as preparation for the future.[15] The names of Lois and Eunice can be added to those of generations of Christians who have effectively instructed and prayed for children and grandchildren, and these two women highlight the importance of Christian nurture in one's family.[16]

Prayer is a foundational activity for parents who desire to see their children follow and serve Jesus long after they leave home. One author noted, "It is never too late to foster the development of character or wisdom in the Lord's servant, yet parents should not forfeit the opportunities of early nurturing."[17]

Paul indicates the importance of the intergenerational character of the mission of the church. His burning issue was how faith can be passed on from one generation to the next. To this point, Paul traces Timothy's spiritual heritage not through his paternal family but through his maternal line.[18] Paul knew the future of the church depended upon the transmission of faith not just from Lois to Eunice to Timothy but from Timothy to the next generation. One author asserted that the development of the next generation of ministry leaders is what captivated Paul's mind and heart while in prison.[19]

Lois and Eunice are credited with the transmission of faith through a "transitional, cross-cultural," and intergenerational replication of Christian faith in the context of "a highly pluralistic, syncretistic, rapidly changing environment."[20] Paul was making a single point in this letter: "Don't lose touch with your roots." Through his letter, Paul insists on the "recollection, the imaginative remembering and reappropriation of apostolic teaching."[21] Paul's reference to Timothy's grandmother and mother regarding the transmission of faith indicates to Timothy that his religious heritage has stability and antiquity.[22] It is faith in Christ that forms the core of Christian character.

One author contends that faith is the ongoing process of response toward God. It is a quality of character, indeed, that can be implanted and nurtured by human relationships and passed down from parent to child. The fidelity shown by parents and teachers toward the young and emulated by the young in the formation of their own character is a critical part of the formation of a theological virtue. It is a virtue that can grow through the stages of a person's life.[23] The teaching source for this faith for Timothy was Lois and Eunice in the domestic sphere rather than the assembly of the faith community. Paul recognized these women as capable teachers who could teach the truth and who could teach faith to others. Paul also recognized the key role of personal witness and nurture in the forming of faithful persons.[24]

Paul did not lay the responsibility of faith formation of the next generation on the local church. Rather, the primary responsibility of socializing faith was to be conducted in households and families. Grandparents and parents are the most important formative influences in a child's life and in the transmission of faith.[25] It is the formation of character in the first-century home that must have contributed to the development of strong families and effective citizens. Could this be the exception Zimmerman referred to as a key contributor to the stabilization of society in the first century?

Thom Wolf may have an answer to Zimmerman's exception of the Christian church for the stabilization of society. Wolf labeled this core teaching *oikoscode*, which is also referred to as the " 'paraenesis' (Greek for advice or exhortation, especially of a moral or spiritual nature; and ethical teaching)." He identified the term "household code" and the German term *Haustafeln* (house-tablets) used technically to refer to social codes of three primary relationships of wife-husband, children-parents, and slaves-masters. Wolf described this code as the " 'threefold structure of ethico-religious teaching' or the 'worldview' or 'pattern of thought.' " The code teaches followers of Jesus a new way of living in society following the ethical teachings and way of life in Christ.[26] The teachings of Jesus imitated by Paul, then learned and lived by Timothy, and taught by his grandmother Lois and his mother, Eunice, demonstrate how families can flourish in faith and contribute to the flourishing of human societies. Paul encouraged Timothy to fan into flame the gift of God on Timothy through the laying on of Paul's hands. He reminded Timothy that God had not given him a spirit of timidity but a spirit of power, of love, and of self-discipline.

The faith formed in Timothy by his family and by the apostle Paul produced a first-century community leader, pastor, and author who could develop another generation of leaders for local churches. Lois and Eunice were integral agents in his development of faith. Paul was another key agent in the formation of this young leader and pastor. Timothy's family is one example of a flourishing family of faith in the first century. The faith formed in Timothy carried the way of life in Christ taught by Paul and an ethical base from the teachings of Jesus. Paul commended Timothy to churches as a living example of this way of life in Christ. This kind of community leader adds value for the flourishing of communities and societies.

Principles of Family Hope

The story of Lois, Eunice, and Timothy generates several principles of family hope such as spiritual formation, faith formation in complex situations, the value of faith stories, the role of women and men in faith formation, the role of the church in flourishing families, and character formation for children and grandchildren.

Spiritual Formation at Home. The spiritual formation of children begins in the home. Lois and Eunice placed a priority on teaching the Scriptures to Timothy as a child. Timothy grew not only with the teaching of Scriptures but also the embodiment of those teachings in everyday lived experience. He saw the power of the gospel in action through normal family life every day. When the faith of parents and grandparents is vibrant, alive, and visible, children and grandchildren notice and learn by observation.

Faith Flourishes in Complexity. Families often face uncertainty, turbulence, and chaos, and yet these scenarios create complex situations in which personal faith can flourish. Timothy's family was in transition from Jewish tradition to Christian faith. Timothy's family was crosscultural, mixing Jewish and Greek culture. The faith passed on to Timothy was intergenerational, spanning four generations, including those he would disciple and develop.

Faith Stories. Telling and retelling the story of faith in families is monumental in the development of religious heritage and legacy. Children and grandchildren want to know their spiritual history and heritage. Retelling these stories serves to memorialize the work of faith in the family's past, present, and future.

Women in Faith Formation. Women nurture children through care and support. They have a unique ability to shape the faith of their children and grandchildren. Women take a lead role in the development of a child including health, nutrition, well-being, protection, nurture, education, and spiritual formation. Forming faith in children and grandchildren is a high privilege and responsibility for women in the family. Mothers and grandmothers pray for their children and grandchildren as a labor of love. Single mothers have the potential to form faith in their children and should be supported by local churches and ministries to help them succeed.

Men in Faith Formation. Men are also critical in the formation of faith in the family. They provide safety, security, protection, and resources for the well-being of the family. The presence of a father in the formation of faith is equally important to that of women in the family. In the absence of a father, another male role model is needed to demonstrate and form faith in a disciple. The spiritual formation and religious education of children and grandchildren is also a priority for men in the family. Fathers and grandfathers pray for their children and grandchildren as a labor of love. Single fathers have potential to form faith in their children, provided they receive support from their church and local ministries. The physical and spiritual absence of fathers in families continues to be a major dilemma of modern society.

Church and the Flourishing Family. Churches and communities of faith are critical to the formation of faith. Churches form a supplemental support for faith formation in the home in addition to the primary role of parents in faith formation. Religious education programs for children should augment what is taught and modeled at home. Churches may feel the pressure of an expectation to provide faith formation intended for the domestic sphere. One option a church might consider is to provide training and support to parents and grandparents for shaping faith in children and grandchildren at home.

Character Formation at Home. When faith is formed in children and grandchildren, future leaders and citizens learn the basic pattern of Christ-centered living and values. They learn lessons of integrity, honesty, repentance, forgiveness, conflict resolution, grace, mercy, respect for the individual, dignity, honor, and most important, they learn how to have a relationship with God through Jesus Christ. The primary location for character to be formed is the home. The best teacher of faith is the example children see in the home every day. Faith is caught more powerfully than taught.

Summary

The story of Lois, Eunice, and Timothy renders valuable lessons for families in the twenty-first century. Parents and grandparents play a critical role in the faith formation of children and grandchildren. They also contribute to the flourishing of families and societies. The transmission of faith to the next generation rests in the hands of parents and grandparents. The effective transmission of faith is the daily embodiment of teaching in the normal ebb and flow of family life. The development of leaders for the church and community rests in the hands of parents in the home. Churches play a crucial role in supplementing spiritual formation led by parents and providing support and resources needed for families in this sacred role.

Questions for Reflection

1. Who formed the Christian faith in you?
2. What is the story of faith heritage in your family?
3. What kind of opportunities are available at home to form faith in children and grandchildren?
4. What are ways to teach the Scriptures and live out its truth among your children and youth at home?
5. What do you need from your church to successfully form faith in your family?

Part 2

Family Solutions

A Prescription for Healthy Families

In the previous ten chapters, we've taken a close-up view of families in the Bible and what we might learn from them. The stories reveal the need for redemption, a redeemer, and an opportunity for grace, forgiveness, and restoration. The goal was to explore the unit of organization chosen by God for humanity—the family—and examine the story of each family to glean important lessons and to learn how God's plan for humanity was worked out through families even when they went astray.

The story of the Divine Family pointed out how the prototype for the human family was already in motion before time began. The relationship between Father, Son, and Spirit outlined a pattern for human relationships in the family. We see distinct roles of each person combined into one God. We see cooperation, harmony, collaboration, and trust in these relationships.

The story of the First Family began with a worship experience that ended in the first murder recorded in human history. So many things went wrong in the first human family, and yet God offered grace, redemption, and a future for Cain even after he murdered his brother. From the First Family, we learn that family conflict is inevitable. The issue is not whether families will have conflict but how they will resolve it. Another painful lesson from this story is that wrong decisions have consequences. Some consequences create permanent damage even as grace and forgiveness are offered and accepted.

The story of the Promised Family demonstrated God's faithfulness to bless humanity through one family, even with its flaws and shortcomings. Abraham's family was far from perfect, yet he was full of faith and willingness to obey God and follow his guidance. This story shows how God's plan allows for human agency, human error, impatience, and self-interest while accentuating God's guidance and grace in human families. The story unfolds with Isaac and then Jacob and Esau for a lesson in sibling rivalry. The need and opportunity for forgiveness, healing, and restoration of family members is abundantly clear.

The story of the Redeeming Family shows us how God works through families, specifically through Joseph's family. The themes of unjust treatment and of sibling rivalry permeate this story, and yet God's purposes remain constant through pain, hurt, jealousy, slavery, injustice, and mistreatment.

The story of the Liberating Family reveals how adoptive families and families of origin can be instrumental in the redemptive plan of God for his people. The issues of crosscultural learning and language form part of God's design to use an emerging and imperfect leader in the plan of redemption.

The story of the Royal Family reveals how the families of leaders are also filled with pain, disappointment, sin, and shortcomings. No parent is perfect. Said another way, all parents are flawed with a sin nature and need God's grace and guidance to be the best parent possible. Parental shortcomings will usually impact the formation of a child even into adulthood. This is another reason we need God's grace, mercy, guidance, and wisdom in rearing children. Children of leaders whom God uses often struggle with their own purpose in life. Even so, seeking God's plan for one's life is essential for meaningful living. God's plan for leading his people continues even through flawed families.

Stories of families in the New Testament are also helpful. The story of the Holy Family is not a story of a perfect family even with Jesus in the middle of it. While Jesus lived a sinless life, his family members were as human and as fragile as we are today. This story is a fascinating review of what it must have been like to live and grow up with God's son within the context of a human family. The story of the Transformed Family provides much hope for families who rise above their circumstances when the power of the gospel takes root. The family gets a new father and new relationships fashioned after grace, forgiveness, servanthood, and the new life available in Christ. Finally, the story of the Flourishing Family provides a clear example of how families are transformed across generations when faithfulness to the gospel message of salvation is taught across three generations. There is no other transgenerational and transformational power stronger than the impact of the gospel in a family.

After reviewing these families of the Bible, I conclude all families are flawed and in need of God's intervention to experience the design intended from the beginning. Human families are flawed but not beyond repair, restoration, redemption, and divine purpose. The family, even with its flaws and imperfections, is still God's design for humanity. As families make room in their circle for the presence of God, the Word of God, and the Spirit of God, they have the potential to become a beautiful picture of healthy relationships, redemption, and purposeful living in God's redemptive plan for humanity. The human family has the potential of reflecting the characteristics of the Divine Family, filled with harmony, cooperation, collaboration, and peace. The family is the laboratory for God's grace. How can we take the lessons learned from these families and implement them into the lives of contemporary families?

In part 2, I am shifting my approach by exploring how a 145-year-old ministry among vulnerable children and families continues to explore new ways of serving families: Buckner International, founded in 1879 by Dr. Robert Cooke Buckner. He was a Baptist pastor from Tennessee who served in Albany, Kentucky, and settled in Texas for most of his ministry. In the beginning of his ministry, Buckner was driven by a passage of scripture framed by James, the half-brother of Jesus, who wrote: "Religion that God our Father accepts as pure and faultless is this: to look after orphans and widows in their distress and to keep oneself from being polluted by the world" (James 1:27).

From the beginning, Buckner had a biblical vision for the care of orphans and widows. Aerial photos of the original campus Buckner purchased in 1880 reveal a row of homes for widows who served as matrons of the children who lived in the orphanage. In its inception, Buckner carried out both objects of James's teaching, providing care for orphans and widows in their distress. Not until 1954 did formal care for aging adults emerge as part of Buckner ministry in Dallas, Texas, with the founding of Buckner Retirement Village. Since the impetus for this ministry was derived directly from the Scriptures, it should not be unique to the ministry of Buckner. The same admonition and teaching from the letter of James is for all

Christian churches and people throughout history. My hope is that the Buckner story will move pastors, ministry leaders, churches, and religious groups of every kind to take up the teaching of James to pursue the practice of pure and faultless religion accepted by God.

Fourteen decades of ministry among orphans, vulnerable children, families, and seniors have taught us many lessons in service. While our methods have changed, our mission remains to follow the example of Jesus in serving vulnerable children, families, and seniors. Chapter 12 documents the story of the Buckner Family Hope Center, which has become a seismic shift in child welfare. Chapter 13 details the story of how Buckner International impacted child welfare practices in Guatemala and gained international acclaim for best practices while following the example of Jesus in serving children. Chapter 14 reflects how the story of Buckner ministry began, where we are today, and a preview of where we are headed with regard to hope for children and families in the twenty-first century.

On the day I was elected unanimously by the Buckner Board of Trustees as the sixth president of Buckner International, my predecessor, Dr. Kenneth L. Hall, presented two gifts to me, commemorating the transition in leadership for this ministry. The first gift was a copy of *R. C. Buckner's Life of Faith and Works*, signed by previous presidents of Buckner International. The second gift was a framed photo of the last building Dr. Buckner built on the historic Buckner Orphan's Home campus in Dallas, Texas, after a wrecking crane smashed into it. Dr. Hall said, "Buckner is still here because we never have been afraid to change." These last three chapters document some of the ways we have changed and pursued best practices and global standards to serve the needs of children, families, and seniors in the twenty-first century.

Chapter 12

THE THRIVING FAMILY

Engaged, Equipped, and Elevated

Do not be conformed to this present world, but be
transformed by the renewing of your mind, so that you
may test and approve what is the will of God—what is
good and well-pleasing and perfect.

—Romans 12:2 (NET)

Thom Wolf, educational entrepreneur and global leadership consultant, taught me a concept that has become a powerful tool in my arsenal of leadership practice: the power of a question. Wolf says there is inherent power in a good question. The person hearing it may not answer it verbally, but they will always answer it in their heart immediately. I also learned that when in conflict or when facing a problem, it is usually better to ask a question before making a statement. Asking a question is one way of engaging in wonderment, the what-if questions of our work. Wonderment leads to imagination; imagination leads to creativity. Creativity coupled with courage and risk, leads to innovation. Innovation leads to breakthroughs and a potential paradigm shift. This kind of thinking became a staple of ministry at Buckner over the past fourteen decades.

The most challenging problems tend to give way to the best questions. Randy Daniels, longtime social work veteran at Buckner International, pinpointed the central problem facing parents of children in developing countries. He concluded, "The number one reason children have been placed out of their homes in the world is poverty."[1] Parents who did not have the economic means to provide for their children felt the only option available to them was to place their children in an orphanage where they would at least have meals, clothing, and basic needs. Daniels began to ask, "What is the solution to this problem? How can we provide these parents with other options that prevent the separation of their children?" That question later developed into a broader question: "What if we were to reach out to families before they reach out to us?"[2] At the time these questions emerged, Daniels noted there were eight million children in orphanages on any given day and two million of these children have no family.[3] Something had to be done. These kinds of insights arose from new experiences through Buckner in international contexts. The beginning of Buckner ministry in international contexts began to influence Buckner, the organization, its ministry, and identity.

Buckner International

The historic name of Buckner was Buckner Baptist Benevolences. However, as the ministry began to address global concerns, the ministry took on an international footprint. Buckner ministry in international contexts began in 1995 when Dr. Hall and Mike Douris, former Buckner staffer and founder of Orphan Outreach, traveled to Poland, Romania, and Russia to research adoption possibilities. Buckner facilitated its first adoption from St. Petersburg, Russia, for a Texas family. By 1996, Buckner created a separate arm for international ministry called Buckner International Ministries to provide humanitarian aid and professional assistance to Russian orphanages. Buckner Shoes for Orphan Souls, formerly Shoes for Russian Souls, originated as a ministry of Dallas Christian Radio KCBI and expanded to shoe drives in fifty states in the USA. Since the beginning of this ministry, Buckner has collected four million pairs of new shoes and distributed them in over ninety countries.[4] By 2004, this movement of humanitarian aid expanded into thirty-two mission trips to seven countries.

Jeff Jones transferred to Buckner Orphan Care International, the new name for the international ministry, and led the way for missions and humanitarian aid to international locations. As Jeff Jones and Randy Daniels worked at the spearhead of innovation, they began to bounce creative solutions between each other, focused on answering the questions Daniels posed. Between 2002 and 2005 Buckner began in-country work in China, Guatemala, Kenya, Latvia, Peru, Ethiopia, Mexico, Honduras, Dominican Republic, Sierra Leone, and Egypt.[5]

Acknowledging the global impact of Buckner ministry, the Board of Trustees renamed Buckner Baptist Benevolences to Buckner International in 2003, under the leadership of the fifth president of Buckner, Dr. Kenneth L. Hall. The shift to international humanitarian aid and in-country ministry provided new platforms to serve the needs of vulnerable children, to develop new approaches to big problems, and to challenge our own best practices in child welfare developed over decades of innovation and change.

Paradigm Shift

Throughout 2005 and 2006, Daniels chronicled

an intentional shift away from pure orphanage support to prevention. He developed a new model of ministry among vulnerable children first pioneered in Russia and Guatemala through the establishment of transitional homes. But soon the international team birthed a new model of ministry in the small town of Tarnevini, Romania. In 2006 Russ Dilday and Randy Daniels travelled with three staff members of Red Dot Buildings based in Athens, Texas, to look at ministry options in Tarnevini. Tarnevini, once an industrial center, was in severe decline. The town was filled with buildings once used as factories but now filled with squatting Roma Gypsy families.[6]

After a review of the situation, Daniels introduced the idea of a Community Development Center and a plan to transform a windowless, barren concrete building into a thriving ministry center for children and families. As the model grew, so did the number of services available. The support of Red Dot Buildings made it possible to develop our first Community Development Center in Tarnevini, Romania. The model was renamed Community Transformation Center and more locations were added in Guatemala, Ethiopia, and the Dominican Republic.[7]

The model was so effective in preserving families and preventing the separation of children from their families that the model was imported from Guatemala to Texas. We were able to strengthen families and help them stabilize financially. Community Transformation Centers provide a wide array of customized services for families to help them gain strength and success as a family. Vocational training, parenting skills, English as a second language, humanitarian aid, and medical services where applicable were added to the menu of services provided. The model quickly spread across the Buckner system domestically and internationally. A new model of ministry quickly emerged, but what was needed was a foundational framework and perhaps a new name.

Protective Factors and Family Hope

By 2015, the Buckner Children and Family Services team adopted a Protective Factors Framework to provide structure and guidance to our emerging model. This framework included five factors every family needs to prevent child abuse and neglect. The five factors are parental resilience, social connections, knowledge of parenting and child development, concrete support in times of need (social connections), and social and emotional competence of children.[8] The framework became the backdrop for organizing the type of services we provided to families. In 2016, we recognized the need to formulate our new model into terms our colleagues, donors, and supporters could clearly understand.

By 2016, our promotional material began to reflect the new language our colleagues developed. We noted one in four children in our state was living in poverty. We changed the name of our Community Transformation Centers to Family Hope Centers.[9] Transforming a community was a broader vision to change a community at the macro level. We were focused on serving, preserving, and strengthening families, therefore impacting the community at the micro level. Rather than transform a community, we were focused on providing hope to families with tangible solutions to their greatest challenges. We divided Family Hope Center work into three phases: engaging families, equipping families, and elevating families.

Engaging Families

Engaging families means we provide family assistance and community events to meet families and serve them at the point of their needs. Engaging families means we provide concrete assistance in a timely fashion through youth and community events. Community events might include health fairs, family assistance, summer camps, sports camps and sports leagues, seminars, and training sessions.

These events are promoted widely in the community as well as by word of mouth. Once families are engaged, we are able to tell them about other services available. Volunteers from local churches provide the human resources and expertise needed to provide a high level of excellence and a positive experience for families who participate. Families voluntarily responded to equipping opportunities.

Equipping Families

Equipping families means offering parent education, adult education, financial empowerment classes, child and youth development activities, and spiritual development. Adult education classes include English as a second language, general education diploma for high school education, literacy classes, and life skills. Financial empowerment might include job skills training, vocational training, financial management, and income-generating activities. Child and youth development includes after-school programs, a youth academy summer program, mentoring, and at international locations, might include formal school education.

Elevating Families

Elevating families is accomplished through family coaching, counseling, and spiritual enrichment.[10] We changed our labeling of working with families from clinical management to family coaching, a more family-friendly approach. We explained that even our favorite professional athlete had a coach. Families needed coaches, too, to improve and succeed. Community involvement and leadership is also encouraged through coaching of families.

Kimberly Allen and Nichole Huff published the first known research on the concept of family coaching in 2014. They concluded that "family coaches strive to create coach-client partnerships that offer support and cultivate growth opportunities through the use of coaching techniques and models."[11] They also found that family functioning improves when the intervening professionals use coaching techniques.[12] Buckner Family Hope Centers feature two family coaches managing a maximum of fifty families supported by a director, a child and youth specialist, and a community services coordinator.

Today, Family Hope Centers across Texas are provided in Lubbock, Midland, Dallas, Longview, Houston, and the Rio Grande Valley as well as in cities throughout Peru, Honduras, Guatemala, Mexico, the Dominican Republic, and Kenya. Family Hope Centers in these locations are strengthening families and preventing abuse and neglect through contextually appropriate solutions. The result is that children remain in the families where God put them. They can grow, learn, and develop in their family of origin. We continue to provide Family Hope Centers with funding from donors without government funding. Buckner Family Hope Centers are not only providing hope for families but also changing the face of child welfare practice in the United States and abroad. All this work is possible through the generosity of donors.

Disruption to Innovation

Most nonprofit organizations exist to respond to a tragedy, a need, or a social situation with solutions and resources. Yet, few nonprofit organizations work upstream to get to the root of the problem. A Family Hope Center became a disruption to our own best practices in foster care, adoption, and single-parent support programs, while helping families remain intact and succeed so they don't need these services. We began reaching families before they reached out to us. We continue to offer reactive services while providing a proactive service to strengthen families.

National leaders in child welfare noticed the difference we were making. Kathleen Strotman, former Executive Director of the Congressional Coalition on Adoption Institute, addressed the Buckner International Board and said, "Buckner is alone in this space of family preservation."[13] Jedd Medefind, President and CEO of the Christian Alliance for Orphans (CAFO) also spoke to the Buckner International Board and said, "I know of no other nonprofit organization affiliated with CAFO that is doing this kind of work."[14] We continued to innovate and develop Family Hope Centers and have plans to add more in the near future. This solution set for families not only strengthened and helped families succeed, but there were also economic benefits.

An Ounce of Prevention

You have heard "an ounce of prevention is worth a pound of cure." One of our major donors and friend of Buckner challenged me to make a financial case for effectiveness and funding of Family Hope Center. I took up his challenge and commissioned a study to inquire into the difference between foster care initiated by the State of Texas and outsourced to Buckner Children and Family Services compared to the work of Buckner Family Hope Centers. I asked Kandyce Ormes Ripley, associate vice president of data analysis and strategy at Buckner, to dig into the data on foster care. I asked her calculate the cost of hiring a child protective services representative in the state of Texas with compensation and benefits, the cost of training, the cost of an investigation of child abuse, neglect, or abandonment, the cost of reporting the results, the removal of a child from his or her family, the recruitment, orientation, training, and certification of a foster family, the placement of the child, and then subsequent monitoring needed, and the reporting requirements for this placement for one year.

The total cost added up to $54,000 for one child for one year. This total would include costs provided by taxpayers and Buckner donors. Then I asked her to calculate the cost of family coaching in a Family Hope Center that resulted in a child remaining in their family. In other words, the cost of preventing a child from being separated from his or her family due to neglect, abuse, or abandonment. The total cost of family coaching for one year added up to $2,000 provided by private donations. The ratio of prevention to cure was one to twenty-seven. In other words, for every dollar we spent on prevention, we would have to spend twenty-seven dollars after abuse, neglect, or abandonment was reported. The case was compelling. We know this is right. We know this is true. "An ounce of prevention is worth a pound of cure." I did not add the costs of lifelong effects of the traumatic experience of abuse, abandonment, neglect, or separation from one's family. The work of Family Hope Centers is an outstanding investment in child welfare. We are convinced. Are you?

Back to the Future

The last time I traveled internationally on behalf of Buckner was in January 2020 with a group of Buckner donors. Then in the summer of 2022, I traveled to Guatemala to visit two Family Hope Centers and our foster care ministry there. It was my first international trip since the start of the pandemic, and it reminded me how much I missed the opportunity to meet the people we serve and spend time with our teams outside the US. This time I had a group of Texas leaders with me to experience the ministry firsthand. Tony Celelli, president of Stark College and Seminary; Abe Jaquez, president of Baptist University of the Americas; Brian Hill, senior pastor, First Baptist Church of Corpus Christi; Tamiko Jones, executive director of the Woman's Missionary Union of Texas; and Irene

Gallegos, director, Hunger and Care Ministries, Center for Cultural Engagement for Texas Baptists, accompanied me for a blockbuster week with Buckner staff. I was reminded again of the scope of our work and the direct impact we're having on the lives of children and families.

As I stood on the roof of the Buckner Family Hope Center in Jocotenango, Guatemala, I was struck by my two views. Looking up and out, we were surrounded by beautiful green hills cloaked in a vast array of vegetation, a symbol of the strength of Guatemala's soil. Looking down, however, was a completely different view. As beautiful as the natural surroundings were, the Family Hope Center was also surrounded by poverty and desperation. This was the first Family Hope Center started by Buckner. It was in Jocotenango where the idea germinated into nearly thirty Family Hope Centers internationally and in Texas. These life-changing centers are strengthening families, enabling them to keep children where they belong, in the home. We are transforming countless generations to come, breaking cycles of poor parenting and shining hope for boys and girls.

As systems change domestically and internationally, it is becoming increasingly apparent that family preservation programs like those offered at the Family Hope Center are vital to the future of serving vulnerable children. During my time in Guatemala, we had the opportunity to visit families being served by Buckner. We walked to their homes, often through devastating poverty. Regardless of the surroundings, we found change and hope inside each home. Undeterred by the challenges facing them, these families, while different, have the same story. Buckner is providing hope and promise for them. In some cases, it's financial training and parenting classes. In other situations, it's a combination of new shoes, food supplements, water filters, and family strengthening through training.

I had the wonderful privilege of meeting Valentina, a young girl who frequents the Family Hope Center in Jocotenango. Her mother told me she learned it was best to talk to her daughter and reason with her rather than hit her out of frustration. Through equipping experiences and learning parenting skills, Valentina has a trans-formed mom who supports her dream to become an engineer. Valentina is a bright young lady with dreams, aspirations, and a hopeful future. She has a mother and father who see her potential and are ready to support her in her educational journey toward her dream vocation. Valentina represents the thousands of girls and boys who have goals, dreams, and hopes that can become a reality with parents who value, respect, and support them.

One dimension of the Buckner Family Hope Center in Jocotenango is the engagement with children in a nearby elementary school. Our Buckner leaders met with the principal of the school, who agreed to host a Buckner Day at the beginning of their school year. The team that traveled with me participated in backpack and shoe distribution. I had the opportunity to share a backpack full of school supplies and a pair of brand-new tennis shoes with one of the students. I will never forget the look on the face of the girl sitting in front of me when I pulled out the pair of new tennis shoes. Her smile seemed to stretch from ear to ear. I asked permission to remove her socks and shoes. She agreed and allowed me to wash her feet and then place brand-new socks and shoes on her. I worked with her until we got the right size of shoes and ensured they fit perfectly. Then I showed her the backpack and school supplies ready for her to start a new school year. I prayed a blessing over her and off she went.

Meanwhile parents were participating in a cooking demonstration with a professional chef. I got to taste the delicious dish the chef was preparing. Irene Gallegos and Tamiko Jones were at another station teaching a Bible story to another group of children. The teachers at the school also served as volunteers. Our hearts were full of blessing through firsthand serving opportunities. This is what engagement with children and families is like. The next step for some of the families we met may be to sample other services we provide and to enter equipping experiences.

Summary

Buckner Family Hope Centers have blessed families on the brink of dissolution in the United States of America and abroad. This innovation has transformed Buckner to expand from reactive to proactive services for families. International adoption led to international humanitarian aid in orphanages and mission trips to provide orphanage support. These efforts led to in-country services including the innovation of Family Hope Centers to preserve and strengthen families. Buckner leaders were positioned to solve problems, ask questions, and to create innovative solutions to challenges faced by vulnerable children and families. Along the way, there were new opportunities to impact child welfare practices not only of Buckner but also of foreign governments. The next chapter tells the story of how Buckner began to shape, influence, and encourage changes in child welfare practice and policy among nations of the global south.

Chapter 13

THE REMADE FAMILY

Reunification, Kinship and Foster Care, and Adoption

Being a family means you are a part of something very wonderful. It means you will love and be loved for the rest of your life.

—Lisa Weed

The ministry of Buckner started just after the American Civil
War. Many fathers from Texas joined the Confederate Army
to defend slavery and lost their lives. Wives became widows, children
became fatherless. In some cases, widows lost their lives as single
mothers trying to survive and raise a family. Many children became
true orphans with no parents and no family to care for them.

When Robert Cooke Buckner, a Texas Baptist pastor, began
Buckner Orphans Home in Dallas, Texas, in January of 1879, this
ministry became the first orphanage west of the Mississippi River
in the United States. Buckner built a place for children to have a
home and a family.[1] Yet after decades of consistent service among
orphans and vulnerable children housed in an orphanage, Buckner
has transitioned from institutional-based care of children to family-
based care. The whole field of child welfare in the United States
has shifted from orphanage care and residential care in institutions
to families through foster care, kinship care, adoption, and family

services. We believe the best place for a child to grow and develop is a safe and healthy family environment. We have developed fourteen decades of expertise in this field, as well as best practices and service excellence as a practitioner of finding and building forever families for children.

Our guidepost verse and foundational scripture is James 1:27 which says, "Religion that God our Father accepts as pure and faultless is this: to look after orphans and widows in their distress and to keep oneself from being polluted by the world." Commitment to living out this guiding verse in our work has led to an international reputation of excellence in serving vulnerable children and senior adults. James, the half-brother of Jesus, is saying the most acceptable practice of religion in God's sight is doing whatever it takes to look after the needs of orphans and widows, to visit them in their place of need, and to secure a family for them to belong to. This vision led us to an exciting adventure to serve orphans, vulnerable children, and families in international settings that led to global impact for the well-being of children. The story of that journey includes influence in Washington, DC, and then on to the global stage through engagement with a United States Aid and International Development (USAID) grant to transition institutionalized children to families and opportunities to share our expertise.

Buckner International seeks to find families for children rather than children for families. We realize that every child should have a safe family environment in which to grow up. We believe a family is the best place for a child to learn, grow, and develop. Independent young adults who have aged out of foster care need a family as they launch their lives. Foster families, adoptive forever families, kinship families, single-adult families, and traditional families all form basic family units capable of creating a sense of community and belonging for children to be nurtured and loved.

Applying for a USAID Grant

Several years after Dr. Ken Hall, my predecessor, established an office in Washington, DC, to engage the US federal government in international orphan care, I led the ministry to apply for a grant from USAID. Three grants were posted by USAID in Vietnam, Cambodia, and Guatemala. We applied for the Guatemala grant since we had established ministry in that country in the early 2000s. The goal of the grant was to assist the Guatemalan government to transition 103 children, ages birth through three years, from orphanages to families through foster care, kinship care, or adoption.

Margaret Elizabeth Perry McKissack, then director of corporate and institutional relations for Buckner, was the original grant writer and project leader. She assembled a cross-functional team at Buckner to develop the grant and launch the project. After a first rejection of our grant application, we were encouraged to apply again. Margaret Elizabeth enlisted a consultant and made a second attempt to successfully win a $1 million dollar grant over a two-year period. Our first USAID grant for $1 million dollars was awarded on August 1, 2013, to "develop programs in Guatemala that will provide permanent family solutions for orphans and vulnerable children."[2] This grant was cause for a great celebration at Buckner.

The project called for the deinstitutionalization of young children through a permanency team of experts to manage children's cases, training and equipping the Guatemalan government to develop foster care and kinship care programs, and developing a system to manage and track data on children and foster families.[3] In 2013, the concept of foster care, placing a child in temporary custody of a safe and healthy nonbiological family environment, and kinship families were fairly new concepts in many developing countries. Buckner led the way in developing foster care and kinship care in Guatemala as well as other places like Peru, Honduras, Mexico, the Dominican

Republic, Russia, Ethiopia, and Kenya. Randy Daniels, vice president of Buckner Children and Family Services, indicated Guatemalan orphans were automatically placed in an orphanage regardless of age as a standard practice. The project would include an educational component based on the latest research in child welfare.

This project was part of the *USAID Action Plan for Children in Adversity*, the first whole-government strategic guidance on international assistance for children in adversity. The action plan included three principal objectives: *To Build Strong Beginnings* by increasing the percentage of children surviving and reaching full developmental potential; *To Put Family Care First* by reducing the percentage of children living outside of family care; and *To Protect Children* by reducing the percentage of girls and boys exposed to violence and exploitation.[4] Buckner plans for this project were dubbed "Fostering Hope Guatemala" and supported all three objectives.

Since part of the project included developing software and hardware solutions for the Guatemalan government, we engaged a subcontractor to provide these solutions. However, once we began to implement the project, it became apparent the first provider's solutions were incompatible with Guatemalan government computer systems. At every turn, obstacles seemed to emerge. Even so, we kept moving in good faith toward the goal. We became aware of Tyler Technologies, a software solutions company in Plano, Texas, specializing in software for the public sector, including solutions for government court systems. Bruce Graham, then chief strategy officer, connected us to a team of Tyler professionals that provided customized solutions to the challenges we were facing in Guatemala with computer systems.

Through ongoing connections with US senators and leaders on Capitol Hill with a passion for child welfare, we were able to secure the support and encouragement needed to apply for this grant.

Senator Mary Landrieu from Louisiana was incredibly supportive of the Buckner–USAID grant application saying, "Children may make up only about 30 percent of the world's population, but they represent 100 percent of our future."[5] Her vision was for the United States to make critical investments abroad to successfully provide children with opportunities to reach their full potential for a brighter and more secure future.[6]

Project implementation began in 2013 with a contextually appropriate name in Spanish: *Semillas de Esperanza* (Seeds of Hope), providing hope for 103 children and their families. The implementation team was led by Carlos Colón, executive director of international operations for Buckner Children and Family Services. As we began the project, our team members encountered amazing stories of children being separated at birth, several cases of reunifying children with families, and many cases of rediscovering families for children separated from their families for several reasons.

Lost and Found: Baby Sara's Return Home

The story of Baby Sara is an incredible journey of hope. Her name and the names of her family members have been substituted to protect their identity. Dina Tomás was a caseworker for Semillas de Esperanza, and she logged many hours on foot to trace separated families from their children. Due to incomplete files, a backlog of cases, and a rural setting, Dina's casework involved face-to-face investigation. She traveled to a Kekchi Maya village of San José Pacayal checking up on two-year-old Sara, whom she helped reunite with her parents following a bizarre story involving a hospital mix-up, a cover-up, and a search for her family. To get to the village, Dina had to drive on a national highway for six hours before turning onto a dirt road that would take her to a pedestrian suspension bridge and lead her to the trail that would take her to the mountainside village where Sara lives.

Sara was born in April 2012 to Juana Pap and her husband, Bartolo Díaz, at a health center in Chahal. Díaz is an agricultural worker. Pap is a homemaker. Sara was born underweight at three pounds and diagnosed with malnutrition, while her mother was diagnosed with anemia at the hospital. Both were taken to another hospital for treatment, but while Pap was discharged, baby Sara remained for further treatment. Needing specialized care, Sara was transferred to a third hospital, this time in Cóban. Word got back to Mr. Díaz, her father, that his daughter had been transferred, but then her story took a bizarre turn.

When Mr. Díaz found out that his daughter had been transferred to the third hospital, he visited several times, bringing diapers, baby powder, and clothes for his daughter. However, hospital administrators would not let him see her. He returned and later he called, but still they did not let him see his daughter. He kept calling the number of the hospital, and they would not give him any information on his child. Dina explained to hospital administrators that Mr. Díaz could not visit the hospital often because of the family's remote location. The hospital was six hours away with little to no transportation available to him. He rarely went to Cóban but kept calling to no avail. Mr. Díaz spoke of the despair he felt at the time. He became sad about his daughter. Díaz, who works at a palm farm, said he finally gave up because he could not afford to continue the search in Cóban. "If he missed one day of work, he would be fired." Dina said the last time the family called the hospital in Chahal, officials there told them, "The child had passed away." So, he gave up and stopped calling the hospital because, according to them, she had died. Meanwhile, at the hospital, since no family had visited the infant and little information was available on her, the child was declared adoptable by hospital officials. At this point, baby Sara might have been adopted by a family unfamiliar to her. But the story was not over yet.

The Buckner Guatemala Seeds of Hope team intervened in November 2013 to determine Sara's identity and family connections. By April 2014, Dina and the Seeds of Hope team continued the investigation, finally working their way to the initial birth hospital in Chahal. They shared this information on Radio Bendición, a Christian radio station in Chahal, to try to find Sara and find her parents, Juana Pap and Bartolo Díaz. Following leads they received from the hospital, Dina tracked down Sara's parents at San José Pacayal, asking one neighbor after another if they knew Mr. Bartolo and Ms. Juana. They did, guiding her to the couple and their large extended family, who were stunned and overjoyed when Dina brought them the news their youngest daughter was alive.

The visits continued with home studies, hearings, and finally, a reuniting with Sara's large extended family. Mr. Díaz recalled his and his wife's feelings with Dina the moment when she told him his daughter was alive "Ah yes, I felt so calm when you came and told me." For Dina, the successful, though difficult, search was a labor of love for God. "That's what I love about my job, is that I'm serving God," she said. "God is my partner. He is my boss. He sends me to work for the people who need it. I am just an instrument and I have weaknesses, but I want to strengthen them and keep supporting these people." It is a sentiment Díaz emphasized to her. "Many thanks to God. God's blessings on you."[7] The Semillas de Esperanza team worked toward happy endings like Sara's experience. They were able to reunite children with families and celebrated exciting reunions. The Semillas de Esperanza team also discovered a few cases with children who had been kidnapped.

Kidnapped at Birth

Margarita Gomez (substituted name) slowly stirred in a dark room with aches and pains, a day after childbirth. Her hands glided up and down the bed around her, but she could not sense the body of her newborn. Sitting up, she called to those who had been taking care of her and asked for her newborn child. "You have no child, they responded." Gomez knew that was a lie, but her life was threatened if she ever professed otherwise. Her baby was gone. Later that day, Gomez and her two young children boarded a bus that returned her to her quiet Guatemalan village. Throughout the next few days, she relived what happened. Elvia and Mario Sosa (names substituted) promised to help her. They arranged for a doctor to deliver her child. Yet shortly after she arrived at their home, she and her children were locked up. The birth of her son was a blur. She never held, never even saw her boy, Samuel.

Three days after the birth of her son, Gomez reported the situation to the police, launching a nationwide search for Samuel. It began with legal authorities taking Gomez back to Cantel, where she awoke after childbirth. The only thing she remembered was a store right in front of the house. She remembered there were some railings on a little hill, and that's when authorities found the house.

Inside the home, local authorities discovered the Sosas and baby Samuel. Baby Samuel was rescued from the couple that had stolen him. Local authorities arrested the Sosas and placed Samuel into care at Casa Alegria, a children's center, without the love and care of his mother, brothers, and family. Jenifer Montes, a Buckner caseworker with the Semillas de Esperanza project was notified of Gomez's situation by Guatemala's national judicial court. Her assignment was to perform the investigation and legal casework necessary to determine if Gomez was the mother and, if so, reunite her with her baby.

When Jenifer learned the case was a kidnapping, a child ripped out of his mother's arms, and that she did not even get to meet him, she felt three times as committed to her and the baby. Jenifer said this case seemed so unfair and made her feel so powerless since she could not fix it immediately. Jenifer turned to her expertise and to a higher power to tackle the case. When she heard about the case, she asked God to enlighten her mind and to guide her on the right path, leading her to the right people to talk to, and how to best serve the family. The case was the first of its kind for Jenifer with the Semillas de Esperanza project. In Guatemala, there are hundreds, even thousands, of kidnapped children. The children are lost, and the mothers stay silent out of fear or because of a threat or ignorance or not knowing what they can do. In irregular adoptions, the children get sold.

As the kidnapping happened in Quetzaltenango, Guatemala, the investigation process started in a court located within a geographic division. Since Margarita was living in another geographic division, the case was transferred to another court. After a month had passed, there was no information about the family, their address, or why the child was in custody. The longer the case was delayed, the harder and more challenging the investigation became. After interviewing Margarita, Jenifer ordered a DNA test to determine whether she was Samuel's mother. She arranged court hearings for Margarita and Samuel. Seventy-five days after he was placed into state care, a judge granted Margarita provisional care of Samuel.

On a cloudless morning in a quiet village, Samuel returned home with his mother, siblings, uncles, and grandmother. Jenifer displayed a big smile at the sight of his family reunion. She helped Margarita fill out the last of the custody forms to complete the end to her long six-month ordeal. When the DNA test results were positive, Jenifer Montes concluded Samuel's "right to have an identity had been restored." Margarita looked up at Jenifer with a mother's smile and said, "I really appreciate Buckner a lot because they did a really good job. My baby is with me now. I am very happy."[8]

Unfortunately, the Semillas de Esperanza team encountered many of these kinds of cases during the project. Each situation, when resolved, became another moment of hope and celebration. Many of our cases resulted in family reunification, like baby Sara and Samuel. However, in some cases, we were not able to find a child's family of origin, or we were not able to return the child to their biological family. Our goal, as the next best option to reuniting children with their biological families, is to seek a family context and support system to approximate the genuine biological family where each child is wanted, loved, and supported in a healthy family environment. In these situations, we place children with foster families.

Families Marked by Love

The Arroyos' home is marked by love, literally. On the wall outside their front door, they have painted a big red heart surrounded by multicolored handprints belonging to each member of the family. One handprint is noticeably smaller than the rest. It belongs to Valeria, the newest addition to their home.

Francisco Arroyo and his wife, Monica Alquijay, of Guatemala, became foster parents almost by accident. They attended a parent meeting at their daughters' school and came across a brochure about a new program being developed in Guatemala in partnership between the Secretaria de Bienestar Social (Secretary of Social Well-Being), Buckner, and USAID. Francisco and Monica expressed a polite interest in the program while talking with the government representative who was distributing information at the school meeting. They left their contact information with the woman but did not really think anything would come of it. Soon, a social worker called them almost every evening to follow up and discuss the certification process in more detail.

"To be honest, I was afraid in the beginning," Monica said. She and Francisco did not commit right away but did what they always do before making any big decisions—discuss it as a family. They had a meeting with their daughters, Elisa, seventeen, and Allison, twelve, and spent several days discussing their thoughts and feelings, things that might change and challenges the family would face if they agreed to foster. Ultimately, they all agreed to take on this big adventure. The feeling that their family was incomplete was influential in their decision. Monica always wanted to have three kids, but unfortunately, because of health issues, they could not grow their family.

As soon as they made the decision to move forward, Monica felt the same emotions as if she were pregnant. There were exams and tests, interviews with psychologists and lots of nerves in the meantime. Eventually, they were asked to foster a nine-month-old boy. While they were considering it, they got another phone call a few days later asking them to instead take a five-month-old girl who had been abandoned by her biological mother at birth. They had not met the baby, had not seen photos or anything else, but they called and said Francisco and Monica had to decide with little information. "Originally, we wanted a boy because we already have two girls, so we did not know what to do. Then we talked to each other and asked, 'Why are we doing this? We want to do it to help and give a child the opportunity to have a family.'" So, they decided to receive the child.

They picked Valeria up from the courts in a district two hours away the next day. The whole drive there, it was as though Monica was going into labor. She was nauseated and dizzy and overcome by nerves. The moment they saw Valeria, though, they both fell head over heels in love. They returned to a big welcome home party with their extended family.

Everyone has accepted Valeria and treated her as if she were related to them by blood. Monica's cousin gladly supplied the couple with the crib her baby had slept in, and Monica's mother bought new baby outfits. One of Francisco's aunts, a devout Catholic, worked on getting permission to have Valeria baptized in the church even though the Arroyos did not have possession of her birth certificate. Signs of love were everywhere, including Valeria's little space that Monica proudly prepared in one corner of their master bedroom. She and Francisco were proud about how well Valeria is doing with her fine motor skills, how she loves to dance, how intelligent she is, and how she imitates her sisters when they do their schoolwork by pulling out her own storybooks or painting pictures alongside them as they work.

A green clothbound photo album revisits Valeria's first bath in her foster home, her first taste of pureed carrots, her sisters helping her brush her teeth, her first Christmas tree. Though they are well aware that Valeria could be taken and placed elsewhere at any moment, Francisco and Monica are committed to loving and cherishing her as much as they possibly can every moment they have with her. They treat her like their own.[9]

Valeria's story is one example among hundreds of situations we encountered with the goal of transitioning children from an orphanage to a healthy family environment. Some children were lost, separated from their families, and were reunited. Other children were kidnapped, found, and returned to their parents; others were placed in foster families, and still others were adopted into forever families. Once the momentum of the Semillas de Esperanza began to accelerate, the Buckner team hit its stride, and the project became a mission to pursue, a cause to fight for. The results speak for themselves.

Ahead of Schedule, Under Budget, Over the Top

Near the end of the second year of this project, the Buckner team in Guatemala reached beyond the goal of 103 children placed in homes to an apex of 151 placements ahead of schedule and under budget, thanks to Tyler Technologies who contributed the value of their work as a pro bono gift.[10] The results were incredible. Our leaders contacted USAID officials to inquire about where we were to send unused funds. USAID officials responded by saying they had never received this kind of request. USAID authorized a No Cost Extension for the unused funds for Buckner with a four-month extension from July 31, 2015, to November 30, 2015, bringing the project duration to twenty-eight months. The Buckner development team successfully secured a private donation from the Rees-Jones Foundation to extend the project one additional year to fund the extension.

At the end of the twenty-eight-month project, 207 children were transitioned from an institutional placement to family-based care. Of the 207 children placed, 154 were ages birth through three years of age; 53 were four years of age or older. In terms of placements, one child was placed with a community family, thirty children were placed in foster families, sixty children were reunited with their biological families, eighty-eight children were placed in kinship families, and twenty-eight children were placed into adoptive families.[11] The support team included Margaret Elizabeth Perry McKissack, Phil Brinkmeyer, and Chris Cato, while the implementation team included Carlos Colon, Roberto Tejada, and a project manager.

The Buckner Semillas de Esperanza Team and the Buckner Children and Family Services Support Team made history at Buckner International in Guatemala and with USAID for the benefit of orphans, vulnerable children, and families. It was time for nations to celebrate this achievement. The Semillas de Esperanza program was evaluated by an independent consultant with thirty-seven years' experience in international development. The evaluator said, "The Semillas de Esperanza program was completed on time, under budget, and exceeded expectations. Rarely does a complex development program achieve all three of these results."[12]

Protocol Ceremony and Buckner Nation

In May 2015, we celebrated the official culmination of a twenty-eight-month Buckner project in Guatemala funded by a USAID grant to build capacity of the Child Welfare System in Guatemala; to develop child permanency (transferring children from institutional care/orphanages into healthy biological, foster, kinship, and adoptive families); and to enhance the infrastructure for child welfare services. A protocol ceremony was held in Guatemala City with representatives from the Guatemalan government including justices of the supreme court, the attorney general, the executive director of the National Council for Adoption, and the secretary of social well-being (human welfare) in Guatemala City. Roberto Tejada, interim executive director, Buckner Guatemala, and I represented Buckner, and Martin Hayes represented USAID.

Roberto, Martin, and I had the privilege of a private audience with eleven of the thirteen justices of the Guatemalan Supreme Court to thank them for their effort to deinstitutionalize vulnerable children and orphans. I also had the honor of addressing a group of dignitaries, government officials, Buckner Guatemala staff, and media representatives in the supreme court chamber to transfer equipment, software developed by Tyler Technologies, and training manuals to the president of the Guatemalan Supreme Court. The Supreme Court Protocol Ceremony featured the display of the flag of the Guatemalan Supreme Court, the flag of Guatemala, the flag of the United States of America, and the flag of Buckner

International. That day, Buckner became a "nation" shining bright hope on vulnerable children, orphans, and families.

While Buckner Nation is not a sovereign nation-state, it is a place where hope shines bright, a place where children are placed in healthy family environments, and a place where lives are redeemed.[13] The opportunity to execute this project moved Buckner onto the global stage in unique ways. We were fortunate as a nonprofit organization to engage in a collaborative effort involving the US government, the Guatemalan government, and a for-profit company to make life better for children growing up in institutional care and the opportunity to grow up in a family. The efforts and success of Buckner team leaders opened opportunities for Buckner to share best practices in child welfare on a global scale.

BEB and the Global Symposium on Child Permanency

In 2012, I joined the board of directors of Both Ends Burning (BEB), currently known as Both Ends Believing, a nonprofit agency founded by Craig Juntunen to overcome obstacles in international adoption. During a 2014 BEB board meeting, we began to explore our purpose and ways to refine our mission to make a long-lasting impact in child welfare. I shared the Buckner–USAID experience and suggested the group connect with Tyler Technologies for potential collaboration. The leadership team contacted Bruce Graham at Tyler and began discussing potential collaboration to tackle the challenge of identifying children and developing a process to place them in forever families, like the solutions Tyler introduced in Guatemala as part of the Buckner–USAID project.

The BEB–Tyler Technologies relationship blossomed. Today, BEB, in collaboration with Tyler Technologies, has established software solutions, called Children First Software, in four developing countries to register more than seventeen thousand children and put them on the road to placement in a forever family.[14] BEB founder Craig Juntunen created an annual conference called the Global Symposium on Child Permanency and invited government leaders responsible for child welfare from various countries to cast a vision for moving children into families among nations open to learning about best practices in this field.

In 2014, Craig invited me to present Buckner best practices at the BEB Global Symposium on Child Permanency held at Harvard University on November 7, 2014. My presentation, "Not One Orphan Child . . . but all Orphan Children," was presented to approximately seventy-five government leaders responsible for child welfare from various countries. The title for my presentation was adapted from the headstone of Robert Cooke Buckner in Dallas, Texas. He had a big heart for all the orphans in his circle of influence. My assignment was to present Buckner best practices in child permanency and included not only the "what and how?" of our best practices but also the "why?" I used Thom Wolf's Wv^3 Framework to describe cultures and worldviews as context for the Buckner approach.[15]

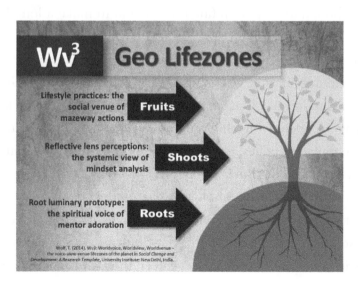

The Wv³ Framework shows how every person has a Mentor, who has a Mindset, a way of analyzing, and a Mazeway, a way of behaving. I then applied the Wv³ Framework to the Buckner Orphan Tree.

The Buckner Orphan Tree identified children in families as the fruit of our work. My goal in this presentation was to explain our root philosophy: the best place for a child to grow and develop is in a safe and healthy family.

The presentation was received with enthusiasm. In fact, the chairperson for the Intercountry Adoption Management Board serving in the Ministry of Women, Children and Social Welfare of Nepal approached me and invited me to come to his country to share the same presentation. He presented me with his business card and added, "When you come to my country, I want you to stay in my home as my personal guest." Knowing the predominant religious expression in Nepal is Hinduism, I asked "Are you sure you want me to come? I will be talking about Buckner ministry and our mentor, Jesus." He said, "Oh yes, Jesus does good work."

The presentation seemed to find a sweet spot in the hearts of social workers and government officials assigned to child welfare.

Since the presentation of Buckner best practices at Harvard University for the BEB Symposium, I have presented this same material in public universities in Peru, Guatemala, and the Dominican Republic. The Buckner Vision for the future of families is a light that shines hope into the lives of orphans and vulnerable children.

Summary

Throughout this experience of the USAID grant in Guatemala, our focus was guided by the biblical witness for the creation and sustainability of family units. We have come to believe and practice the notion that the best place for a child to grow and develop is within a healthy family environment where they are loved, cherished, wanted, and can develop to their full potential. "Children in families" has become our motto. Our discovery and resolution on this truth is born out of the creation model we find in Genesis and throughout the biblical text. Even with the many examples of dysfunctional families in the Bible, we also find the hope and redemptive potential for each family to become all that God intended them to be. While no family is perfect, families can learn how to provide a safe and healthy environment for children to grow, develop, and realize their full potential. When a child finds a family, he or she will love and be loved for a lifetime.

This rich history of best practice in child welfare did not begin in a vacuum. The history of the Buckner legacy has very deep roots. These roots provide a strong foundation for a bright future of family hope, a hope that extends into the twenty-first century. Yet questions remain. How did it all begin? Where are we today? Where are we headed in the future with regard to child welfare, family hope, and better societies where children thrive and prosper? The next chapter seeks to answer those questions.

Chapter 14

FAMILY HOPE

Past, Present, and Future

"For I know the plans I have for you," declares the Lord,
"plans to prosper you and not to harm you, plans
to give you hope and a future."

—Jeremiah 29:11

O ne of the verses most quoted out of context is the promise recorded in Jeremiah 29:11. While the promise is true for all people whose faith rests in a genuine relationship with the resurrected Lord, understanding the context provides deeper and more profound meaning and relevance to the theme of this book.

Family hope was found in the core of this message to the people of God in captivity under King Nebuchadnezzar in Babylon. The people of Israel were forcefully carried away as exiles with their priests, prophets, and leaders of Judah and Jerusalem, including craftsmen and artisans. Yet Nebuchadnezzar did not accomplish this on his own. The prophet records, "This is what the Lord Almighty, the God of Israel, says to all those I carried into exile from Jerusalem to Babylon" (Jeremiah 29:4). The prophet is making the point that God is the mover and shaker of human history. He shapes the events of human history even at the hands of a king who does not honor or acknowledge him. God allowed this to happen and had a purpose and design even during this unthinkable period in the life of his people. This event did not surprise God, although it may have been stunning for his people at that time.

The instructions given to the people of Israel for the next seventy years of captivity focused primarily on the future of the family. The instructions included building houses and settling down, planting gardens for subsistence, building families through marriage and procreation, finding wives for their sons, giving daughters in marriage, and encouraging the growth of their population with grandsons and granddaughters. Instructions were also given for how families should live. These instructions to families included seeking the peace and prosperity of the city to which God carried them and praying for that city and its prosperity. The promise to the people of Israel in captivity for seventy years was that if their new home city prospered, they too would prosper. These promises were bookended with a capstone promise:

> I will come . . . to bring you back. . . . For I know the plans I have for you, . . . plans to prosper you and not to harm you, plans to give you hope and a future. Then you will call upon me and come and pray to me, and I will listen to you. You will seek me and find me when you seek me with all your heart. I will be found by you. (Jeremiah 29:10–14)

My point for the future of family hope is that it is usually in times of crisis, despair, loss, disorientation, and turmoil that we find hope in a God who is present with us, reaching out to us, and available to us with plans for our prosperity and future. The best of family hope becomes accessible in times when we need help the most. What were the seeds of this kind of hope in one of the most challenging crises our nation faced in its history? How has this enduring presence of family hope affected best practices at Buckner today? What does the future hold for family hope for children and struggling families?

How It All Began

The seeds of family hope began in the heart of a young Baptist pastor, Robert Cooke Buckner, in Madisonville, Tennessee. His parents, Daniel and Mary Buckner, were both natives of South Carolina. Daniel was born in 1801 into the home of Henry Buckner, who named Daniel after his friend Daniel Boone. Daniel and Mary married, followed by his ordination to preach in 1823. In 1827 they moved to Madisonville, Tennessee, to plant Ebenezer Baptist Church with twenty-seven members. On January 3, 1833, Robert Cooke Buckner was born into their home.[1]

R. C. Buckner grew up in a pastor's home as well as a missionary's home in Somerset, Kentucky, where his father served as pastor. Buckner attended the Brick Seminary at Somerset and began serving as a minister at the age of seventeen.[2] He also attended Georgetown College in Georgetown, Kentucky, and was later conferred with an honorary doctor of divinity degree by Keachi College in Louisiana and an honorary doctor of law from Baylor University.[3] In 1853, at the age of twenty, R. C. Buckner was called to serve as pastor of the First Baptist Church of Albany, Kentucky.[4] Buckner chose Vienna Long, a member of the First Baptist Church of Albany, to be his wife, and they were married in June 1854.

In that pastoral assignment, Dr. Buckner became close friends with Sam Bell Maxey, a graduate of the United States Military Academy at West Point and an established lawyer, who later became a United States senator. In 1856, Sam Bell Maxey ran for county clerk in Albany. He vowed if he won the election he would remain in Albany. If he lost, he would move to Texas. Maxey lost the election by sixty-six votes and kept his word. Several prominent families including the Longs, Maxeys, Bramlettes, and Crosses moved with him to Texas, all longtime members of the First Baptist Church of Albany. This move became known as the "Great Migration of 1857" from Albany, Kentucky, to Paris, Texas.[5]

Buckner pastored in Salvisa, Kentucky, and in 1859 suffered an attack of typhoid pneumonia. In the fall of 1859, Buckner and his wife moved to Paris, Texas, for him to become pastor of the First Baptist Church of that city.[6] The issue of health played a factor in the Buckner family's move to Texas from Kentucky. The larger factor was that Buckner felt the Lord leading him to begin his pastoral ministry in Texas. This was two years prior to the Civil War in which Texas would side with the Confederacy, defending slavery.

The governor-elect of Texas in 1859 was none other than the famed Alamo hero and prominent Baptist, General Sam Houston. History records the Texas population at six hundred thousand, with 70 percent of the population made up of Anglos and 30 percent made up of African Americans. No mention is recorded of the resident Hispanic population, even though Texas had been part of Mexico only twenty-four years earlier.[7]

For the next twenty years, Buckner served as pastor of the First Baptist Church of Paris, began the *Texas Baptist*, a religious newspaper, and grew his influence among Baptists as they began to form a denomination in Texas. In 1874, he began to publish articles about the toll taken on families by the Civil War conflict. People in Texas were still in grief over the sons and fathers fallen in the war on many battlefields. Buckner began to think about orphans and widows who were left behind and began to ponder the need for an orphan's home. At that time, Dallas was a frontier village on the banks of the Trinity River.

Buckner knew the power of words to rally people to a vision. He wrote these words in an 1876 publication of the *Texas Baptist*:

"Suppose, Brother Deacon, that had been your child and you are dead." With those words, he convened a deacons convention in Paris on July 17, 1877. Deacon Rice Maxey, father of Sam Bell Maxey, presided over the meeting with a gathering of one hundred Baptists from many towns and counties. The assembly voted unanimously to begin the Buckner Orphan's Home in North Texas, and R. C. Buckner was elected as general superintendent. R. C. Buckner, B. H. Carroll, and J. R. Rogers were appointed to a committee to develop a plan.[8] The committee proposed that when $2,000 dollars was in hand, the orphans' home could begin.

The deacons convention was held on a Wednesday, and by the following Sunday, a Sunday school conference was held at First Baptist Church of Paris. On that Sunday, at about one o'clock, a few ministers gathered around an oak tree not far from the meeting house of the conference and gathered the first few dollars. R. C. Buckner said, "Just to give this thing a start," and contributed the first dollar, followed by B. H. Carroll and others until they reached a sum of twenty-seven dollars.

Over the next two years, Buckner raised $1,200 and executed a personal loan for $800 to get started. The Buckner Orphans Home began in Dallas, Texas, on December 2, 1879. Buckner was not content with only telling, preaching, and announcing the good news of the gospel, he was also focused on living out the gospel, especially among the most disadvantaged people in society where he lived. His theology called for the practice of the Great Commission (Matthew 28:19–20) and the Great Commandment (Matthew 22:34–40), both hallmarks of historic Texas Baptist ministry. Buckner soon found a home for orphans by purchasing forty-four acres of land in east Dallas in 1880 and establishing Buckner as the oldest children's charity in the history of Dallas.[9]

Buckner continued to reflect the good news of the gospel for all people by starting the first high school in North Texas for African Americans. He also started the Dallas Humane Society, the Children's Hospital in Dallas, and served as a member of the founding board of trustees of the Baptist Sanitorium, currently known as Baylor Scott & White Health.[10]

In 1914, Buckner, who had served for nineteen consecutive years as the president of the Baptist General Convention of Texas, a volunteer elected role, made a surprising announcement to messengers attending the annual meeting. In that year, he announced at the convention held in Abilene, Texas, that the governance of the Buckner Orphan's Home would be turned over to the Baptist General Convention of Texas.[11] By 1919, after the passing of Dr. R. C. Buckner, the Buckner Orphans Home was serving over six hundred orphans with brothers, Joe and Hal Buckner comanaging the ministry.[12] The next presidents to serve Buckner were also Texas Baptist pastors but not members of the Buckner family: Drs. Ellis Carnett, R. C. Campbell, Kenneth L. Hall, and me.

In 1953, Dr. Carnett filled his time in the first six months of his tenure with raising support for the Buckner Orphans Home in Dallas by visiting twenty-three churches, four encampments, and nineteen Brotherhood, Woman's Missionary Union, and Sunday school convention meetings, usually traveling by car, rail, and bus across 18,500 miles. He wrote twelve letters per day urging Baptist people to pray and make contributions for this vital ministry. By the end of 1953, nearly 3,500 churches gave budget gifts to the ministry and another 1,400 gave a special offering.

The ministry grew with the addition of the Buckner Boy's Ranch near Marble Falls, currently known as Camp Buckner. The first formal expression of senior living was established in the Trew Home in Dallas in 1954, later known as the Buckner Retirement

Village, a home for the aged. Buckner leaders assumed control of the Buckner Baptist Haven in Houston, currently known as Parkway Place, in 1955. In 1957, Buckner opened the Milan Girls Home in Lubbock, Texas.

In 1961, Buckner Trustees made two decisions that further defined the ministry of Buckner. They decided to remove the phrase "Anglo-Saxon Parentage" from their charter so there would be no reference to ethnic group or race, and they changed the name of Buckner Orphans Home to Buckner Baptist Benevolences. By the end of Dr. Carnett's tenure, Buckner operated ministry among children and seniors in Dallas, Houston, San Antonio, Burnet, and Lubbock, Texas. Dr. Carnett retired in 1962 after a decade of growth, expansion, and building.[13]

Dr. Robert Clinton Campbell was elected president in 1963. Among the many innovations introduced by Dr. Campbell, a second foster group home was developed in 1969 in San Antonio in collaboration with Trinity Baptist Church under the leadership of senior pastor, Dr. Buckner Fanning. Trinity Baptist Church members provided spiritual guidance, recreational and educational activities, and many loving families for the children in residence. In addition to human resources and support, the foster group home featured professional services, house parents, and social work by Buckner and material needs by Trinity Baptist Church.[14] In 1970, the Buckner board approved the transfer of two nursing home operations in Austin, Texas, known as the Villa Siesta and the Monte Siesta nursing homes, currently known as Buckner Villas in Austin. Under Dr. Campbell's leadership, Buckner ministry expanded to thirteen locations in Texas, and by 1971, the annual report of ministry recorded services provided to over four thousand individuals with a focus on family rehabilitation for children returning to their family of origin or foster care, adoption, or independent living. That year, 873 children realized this goal.[15]

One of the most historic events during the tenure of Dr. Campbell took place in 1975 when an entire Vietnamese orphanage fled Communist rule and was airlifted to the historic campus of Buckner Children's Home in Dallas. Through many obstacles, barriers, and narrow escapes, sixty-nine orphans from Vietnam arrived in two Greyhound buses to the Buckner campus in Dallas on June 12, 1975.[16] After thirty years at the helm of Buckner, R. C. Campbell announced his decision to retire as the ministry's fourth president in 1992 and served until the end of 1993 to allow the board time to find his successor.

Dr. Kenneth L. Hall was elected by the Buckner board in the fall of 1993 to begin as president of Buckner Baptist Benevolences in January of 1994. His first actions were to launch a twenty-first-century strategic plan and relocate corporate headquarters to downtown Dallas. Another innovation was to lead Buckner to conduct "open adoptions," where public knowledge of birth parents would be available upon request. Dr. Hall coined the phrase "finding families for children rather than finding children for families." Early in his tenure, Dr. Hall led Buckner to expand into international settings and to begin intercountry adoptions from Eastern Europe. In Texas, Hall expanded the ministry of Buckner to Midland, with the transfer of Hearthstone Shelter from the Texas Baptist Children's Home and the addition of a family place, currently known as Family Pathways Ministry in Lufkin, Texas, in collaboration with Angelina Community College by 1996. Family Pathways was a transitional living community with twenty-six apartments for single parents who needed support. In that same year, Buckner added services to families in Amarillo, Texas, including an additional Family Pathways location there.

Dr. Hall led the Buckner board of trustees through the challenge of reconfiguring the historic Buckner Campus with new purposes through a $13 million campaign to raze historic buildings and build new family-like cottages for single parents. Elder care ministries were also expanded to include locations in Longview, relocation in Houston, and a new retirement community in Beaumont, Texas.

Beginning in 2001, Buckner ministry outside of the United States expanded to Romania, Kenya, Russia, Guatemala, Latvia, the Texas border with Mexico, China, Peru, Ethiopia, Honduras, and Mexico. Initially, the ministry in many of these countries focused on orphanage support and included working with government officials and heads of state to improve the condition of orphans and families. The ministry also included intercountry adoptions to the United States. In 2007, the Buckner board voted to change the name of Buckner Baptist Benevolences to Buckner International to reflect the growth and scope of this ministry more accurately.[17]

In 2007, I joined Buckner as president of Buckner Children and Family Services, Incorporated. In 2010 I was elected as the sixth president of Buckner International, and in 2012, after Dr. Hall's retirement, I became president and CEO of Buckner International.

Buckner Today

Family hope at Buckner continues to find its impetus for service in the example of Jesus, who served vulnerable children, families, and seniors. We think of our working from the womb to the tomb, from the beginning to the ending of life and everything in between. The two objects of pure and faultless religion from James 1:27 point to the two areas of focus for Buckner for the past fourteen decades: children and families as well as senior adults. Buckner Retirement Services ventured into the first formal senior living community in Dallas in 1954. As of this writing, our network of senior living communities has expanded to five other locations including San Angelo, Longview, Beaumont, Houston, and Austin. Each of these communities features independent living, assisted living, skilled nursing, and memory care, otherwise known as CCRCs, Continuing Care Retirement Community. This approach to ministry among seniors is to allow the ease of increased needs to be met on the same campus over time and minimize disruption. Senior living is a highly regulated, people-intensive ministry, comprising two-thirds of the Buckner budget and staffing. We believe there is tremendous growth potential to expand our retirement services ministries in the coming years as more and more people age.

Seniors are vulnerable people during the sunset season of their lives. Our theme for these ministry locations is "Inspiring Happiness." Our secret sauce is that we are faith-based. Our mission is to "follow the example of Jesus by serving senior adults." We model our ministry after the example of Jesus, who on the cross, made it a point to entrust the care of his mother into the hands of a nonrelative disciple (John 19:25–27). I encourage our colleagues in retirement services to consider how we engage seniors as if they were our own parents. Each campus features housekeeping, culinary services, activities and events, a wellness center with exercise equipment, chaplain ministry, and a wide range of active living experiences that provide seniors with a flourishing experience as they age. We serve approximately 2,500 senior adults aged sixty-two and older.

The other part of James's teaching is focused on orphans. While Buckner was the first orphanage west of the Mississippi River in the United States, we no longer consider ourselves as an institutional form of care for children. Rather, we have adopted a philosophy that the best place for a child to learn, grow, and develop is in a family. We reduced sixty-four service offerings to three. The "Big Three" include foster care and adoption, Buckner Family Pathways, and Buckner Family Hope Centers. Our mission is to "follow the example of Jesus by serving vulnerable children and families." The focus of our work is ensuring that children grow up in a healthy and safe family. Foster care is provided in collaboration with the state of Texas through the Department of Family and Protective Services. DFPS outsources foster care placements with Buckner as one of many licensed placing agencies. When abuse, abandonment, or neglect is reported to DFPS, the state engages agencies such as Buckner for support. Approximately 601 children were placed in foster care, and one hundred children were adopted through Buckner Children and Family Services across nine locations in Texas in 2022.

Our goal is the reunification of a child in foster care with their family of origin. However, in many cases this is not possible. If a child is not able to return to her or his family of origin, a forever family may consider adoption for a child prior to aging out of the Texas foster care system. Buckner works closely with local churches to identify potential foster parents and invites them to an information meeting, training sessions, and activities that lead them to certification and a formal placement. Buckner staff assist families along the process and continue support after the placement to ensure a positive experience for the child and family. The latest innovation in this field of work is the integration of "trauma informed care" to help families understand the trauma children face through family disruption and placement. We feature a wide range of state-funded prevention programs to help families remain healthy and avoid separation from their children. We also began a donor-funded program called Next Step, for youth between the ages of eighteen and twenty-two who need assistance after they age out of foster care to transition to adulthood and independent living.

Family Pathways is a program for single parents, both female and male, which provides an educational bridge and support to independent living. Single-parent families sometimes face economic challenges, homelessness, and on occasion, domestic violence and disruption, so they need critical help to stabilize. Family Pathways is a campus-based program that provides housing, access to education through a local community college, and family support for parents with children. The goal for this two-year program is for parents to obtain an associate of arts degree in a field of their choice, to gain financial education, to find a vocational opportunity, and to transition to independent living. Other services include counseling through a licensed professional counselor, coaching, and mentoring toward independence. In some cases, clients continue the program through the achievement of a bachelor of arts or science degree, and some exceptions include attainment of a master's degree. In 2022, we provided these services at seven locations in Texas serving approximately 487 parents and children in 166 families. We celebrated thirty-one graduating families with a 94 percent success rate. We integrate "trauma informed care" into these services to help families overcome generational issues that keep them from being successful as a family. This program keeps children and families out of the foster care system.

Family Hope Centers provide families with the support they need to remain healthy, strong, and thriving before a breakdown occurs. I described how this program began in chapter 12. A Family Hope Center serves families who are fragile but have great potential to succeed. We impacted 19,883 lives through this program in 2022 with a 90 percent success rate for families entering the program at nine locations in Texas. The secret sauce is "family coaching" that provides customized solutions to the needs of each family. We involve local congregations through volunteer opportunities to provide spiritual development activities such as Bible studies, vacation Bible school, and other fun activities to serve disadvantaged families in their community. In many cases, when these families request additional spiritual support and help, they turn to these churches. It is not uncommon for us to experience over three hundred faith commitments each year by people we serve in all our programs.

Internationally, we provide foster care and adoption consultation, transitional home services, humanitarian aid, and Family Hope Center support, referred to as family strengthening. Since 1994, we have collected and distributed over five million pairs of tennis shoes among ninety countries due to the generosity of donors to the Buckner Shoes for Orphan Souls program. Kenyan Child Welfare officials have registered Buckner as a licensed child-placing agency and allowed us to place children in Kenya and supported adoptions in Guatemala and Peru for a total of forty-eight placements in 2022.

Since we are not a licensed child placing agency in the rest of the countries we serve, we provide consultation and support to governments upon request. In some countries, we provide a residential program for female teens aging out of the child welfare system and formal schools due to local needs. The most common form of service we provide internationally is the Family Hope Center. These services are available in Peru, Honduras, Guatemala, Mexico, the Dominican Republic, and Kenya. We serve multiple cities within each country through affiliated nongovernment organizations with independent governing boards and indigenous staff who understand their local culture and language to serve children and families. We provide mission trip opportunities to Buckner volunteers who wish to visit these locations to serve children and families as well as support local Buckner staff. In 2022, the total number of lives impacted by international ministry was 20,611 plus 40,911 served through humanitarian aid for a total of 61,172.

The overall shift in Buckner ministry, both domestic and international, has been to grow deeper in the places where we serve rather than wider. We have purposed our efforts and energy to make a deeper, more profound, and more lasting impact among children and families where we already serve communities rather than less impact over a wider area and geographic location. Yet as we have grown deeper, developed consistent standards, outcome, and impact, we are ready for expansion growth given expansion entry and exit criteria to ensure sustainable expansion. The future is bright for both children and families as well as senior living.

Buckner Future

What will family hope look like across the rest of the twenty-first century? None of us can predict the future, but trends, research, and the work of futurists help us imagine the future of family hope for the years to come. Let's look at what is ahead for the family five, ten, and twenty years from now.

In the next five years, we will experience an increasingly diverse population in the United States and a consistent movement of global migration. Paul Collier, professor of economics at Oxford University, contends that migration is a global phenomenon, not unique to the border between the United States and Mexico. He asserts that young people become aware of a richer life in other places and are desperate to leave by both legal or illegal means. Each exodus from their current living situation represents a triumph of the human spirit, courage, and ingenuity in overcoming obstacles and barriers to get to a place where they can thrive. Paul Collier suggests there is a "clear moral obligation to help very poor people who live in other countries, and allowing some of them to move to rich societies is one way of helping. Yet the obligation to help the poor cannot imply a generalized obligation to permit free movement of people across borders."[18] Indeed, this global migration movement has reached the home state of Buckner International.

Stephen Klineberg, retired professor of sociology at Rice University, documents that "all Houston-area residents are now minorities; all are being called upon to build something that has never existed before in human history: a truly successful, inclusive, equitable, and united multiethnic society, made up of nearly all the ethnicities and all the religions of the world, gathered together in this one remarkable place."[19] Klineberg referred to the shift in population makeup for Houston, for Texas, and for major urban centers in the United States as an "epic demographic transformation" and further remarked that "there is nothing humanly possible that can change this future."[20] The future is here now. We are already experiencing demographic changes in our state and nation.

In the next ten years, rapid changes will continue to change the landscape. The year 2023 marks a ten-year cadence to 2033 when the entire world will be recognizing the two-thousandth anniversary of the death, burial, and resurrection of Jesus Christ of Nazareth. Elijah Brown contends six winds of change looming over the next decade.

Demographic Changes

Demographic changes will impact the entire planet with the global population growing to 9 billion with 1 billion in growth attributed to people aged sixty and over by 2050. Half of the world's population will live in the USA, Brazil, Nigeria, India, Pakistan, China, and Indonesia.

Increased Urbanization

Brown predicts increased urbanization will continue in the next decade and grow from 55 percent in 2020 to 68 percent living in urban centers by 2050. The number of megacities with 10 million or more will grow to thirty-nine with twenty of them in Asia.

Plural and Turbulent Cultures

The next decade will see plural and turbulent cultures emerge. Anger, political conflict, and violence will increase as societies become increasingly secular. The next major culture war will focus on public school education.

Vulnerable Populations and Vulnerable Democracies

Vulnerable populations and vulnerable democracies will continue to proliferate. Each year over 100 million people are forcibly displaced from their homes, resulting in more people migrations than at any other time in human history. Per capita gross domestic product in the USA is $49,000 while only $7,000 in Latin America, widening the imbalance of economic prosperity.

Changed Power and Organizational Dynamics

The future will consist of changed power and organizational dynamics. Command and control centers of authority will decline while community-based organizations with shared purpose will emerge. The most effective organizational leaders of the twenty-first century will build systems of collaboration within their organizations, build networks of collaboration, and leverage those networks to address the most complex challenges of the day. Institutions will have to adapt to collaborative partnerships.

Technology and Artificial Intelligence

The expansion of technology and artificial intelligence in daily life will continue to grow. Content is abundant while wisdom will continue to be scarce.[21] These winds of change are already gathering to form a powerful force in the years ahead.

In the next twenty-five to thirty years, the world as we know it will have radically changed. Mauro Guillén, professor of international management at the Wharton School of the University of Pennsylvania, contends that by 2030

> before we know it, there will be more grandparents than grandchildren in most countries. . . . Asian markets, even excluding Japan, will be so large that the center of gravity of global consumption will shift eastward. . . . The largest generation will be the population above age sixty, which today owns 80 percent of the wealth in the United States and is giving rise to the "gray market." . . . Fewer babies, new generations of people, new middle classes, more wealthy women, urban lifestyles, technological disruption, sharing economy, [and] crypto currencies [will all paint the landscape of a new future unknown to us today.] Simply put, the world as we know it today will be gone by 2030.[22]

Philip Jenkins predicts a world where the center of Christianity will have shifted to the global south: Africa, Asia, and Latin America. He contends that the typical Christian "is a woman living in a village in Nigeria or in a Brazilian *favela*. . . . By 2050 only about one-fifth of the world's 3.2 billion Christians will be non-Hispanic whites. . . . Generally, we can say that many global South Christians are more conservative . . . than are the mainstream churches of the global north."[23]

Futurists say the world is changing over the next five, ten, and twenty-five to thirty years. This new world will require innovative solutions for family hope. My sense is that the family of the future will need hope to survive and thrive in this new future world. They will need unchanging principles and wisdom as a point of reference for success. They will need an agency like Buckner International to lead the way, to help, to be a bridge to the future, and to continue to develop innovative solutions inspired by the example of Jesus and anchored in the timeless principles found in Holy Scripture.

Principles of Family Hope

A review of the past, present, and future of Buckner International provides the opportunity to mark principles and best practices from the depth of this rich history of child welfare and senior living services. How it all began covers fourteen decades, 145 years of faithful service. Even in the present, Buckner International leaders are discovering new lessons for how best to "look after orphans and widows in their distress."

Seeds of Hope. The seed of hope began in the heart of a Baptist pastor focused not only on the proclamation of the gospel but also in the practice of it. R. C. Buckner based his ministry on what he saw in scripture. He spoke, wrote, preached, published, and encouraged everyone around him to repeat the gospel, and he engaged them all to do something about it to bring the kingdom of God near to vulnerable children, families, and seniors. Let us never forget how the seed of God's Word took root in this man's heart, where the seed grew, how it was planted, and how it has multiplied through simple obedience to God's Word.

Strategic Churches. All along the way, pastors and churches took up the call to serve orphans and widows in their communities. Churches and the people in churches made the difference in this ministry. They responded to the vision of serving orphans, children, families, and seniors. This biblical mandate and example of Jesus is as applicable to us today as it was in 1879.

Generosity. The ministry of Buckner would have never gained any traction, much less lasted for this long, had it not been for the generosity of God's people. Business leaders, government leaders, and community-minded people and civic societies have also been instrumental in advancing the common good for disadvantaged citizens. Buckner donors continue to contribute their resources so that, together, we can protect children, strengthen families, transform generations, and serve seniors.

Value Added. The ministry of Buckner has added value to congregations and conventions of churches as it has grown and prospered. Dr. R. C. Buckner served for nineteen consecutive years as president of the Baptist General Convention of Texas and led the convention to stability, unity, and purpose. Buckner continues to add value to Texas Baptists, Baptists across the nation, the global Baptist family affiliated with the Baptist World Alliance, and other like-minded church groups that want to make a difference in the lives of children, families, and seniors. We work with Christian groups of multiple denominations and of no denominational connection.

Buckner Leadership. Buckner has been blessed with presidents who serve the mission of Buckner International along with governing boards who bring their talent, time, and treasure to bear on this precious ministry. Leadership is comprised of executive leadership and governing leadership that carries out fiduciary, generative, and strategic roles to advance the mission of Buckner.

Adaptability. Buckner continues to flourish and provide relevant ministry solutions for orphans, children, families, and seniors because it has never been hesitant to change, adapt, and seek flexible solutions to current problems. Buckner has had the same mission over the years but has been willing to change its methods, its buildings, its geography, its governance, and its name to match the needs of contemporary society.

Biblically Based Solutions. Buckner International has been willing to learn and adapt to current social work science and practice in the context of contemporary social needs and changes while also adhering to a Judeo-Christian worldview and biblical principles to ground its values, mission, and vision. The Bible continues to provide a framework and foundation for all we do in ministry. Our hope emerges from the pages of scripture and a deep and abiding relationship with Jesus Christ, the living Lord.

Vulnerable Children and Struggling Families. The future seems to indicate a growing complexity and new sets of challenges for vulnerable children and struggling families. Access to basic human needs such as food, clothing, shelter, water, and stability will grow and put families at risk of disintegration. This trend will consequently impact more children. Access to economic opportunities for families will also become a challenge further impacting global migration for families seeking a better life, fleeing places where political instability rises, and in some cases fleeing war, famine, and danger.

Buckner International. Buckner began offering services outside of the United States in the 1990s. Today we are in six countries offering an array of services. The demand for service in and beyond Texas in the USA will continue to grow. Demand for Buckner services will also grow in many other countries around the world. The challenge for Buckner will be to determine how to scale growth and position itself to provide services or consultation of best practices in a cost-effective, efficient manner.

Conclusion

FAMILY RESET FOR THE FUTURE

I wrote most of this book during the Covid-19 global pandemic. This season of human history has proven to be a time unlike any other across the span of my lifetime. The pandemic sent us back home to our families without notice, without warning, without time to prepare. Within a few weeks, we became isolated. Working remotely from home was a new venture that only a few innovative companies had tried. Buckner had already ventured into these waters on a limited basis. Covid-19 changed this practice for many of our colleagues, except for those assigned to senior living. Families were put to the test. Moms and dads had to reconfigure how they manage work life and family life. New fears and concerns were introduced. Children remained at home and most of them were forced to go to school at home. Parents were faced with new realities, new pressures, new fears, new concerns, and new family patterns and pathways. To quote the words of Dr. Rick Warren, "Covid is a major Re-set for all of us. We are not going back to the past."[1] This reset provides many new opportunities to remake our lives for the new future ahead of us.

This writing project led me into the text of Holy Scripture to rediscover the lived experience of the families of the Bible. I must admit the journey was full of shocks and surprises. As I used the microscope of in-depth biblical research, I was disappointed, frustrated, hopeful, and encouraged as I explored the stories of the families of the Bible. I came to realize that all human families are flawed, to some degree dysfunctional, and in need of a redeemer. And yet our human shortcomings at being a family still do not negate the Creator's choice of the family as the basic organizing principle for humanity. Many of the lessons I found were lessons warning us what we should not do. Some of the lessons were shining examples of what good, strong, healthy families do. All the lessons were helpful to me personally, and I trust will be helpful to your family.

There is hope for the family today. The families of the Bible provide help, hope, and a design for family life. I had to face the humanity of the families of the Bible to discover God's design for humanity. We also must face the humanity of our own families. We must come face-to-face with our own shortcomings and be willing to reach out to the Redeemer of human history for help, guidance, instruction, wisdom, and blessing.

Toward that end, part 2 of this book was intended to describe what Buckner International has done and is doing to shine hope into the lives of families and to inspire happiness among senior adults yesterday, today, and tomorrow. Part of my reason for including these chapters was to document the story and the history of innovation in the service of children, families, and seniors. Buckner is still here because we are not afraid to change. In the next season of our history, we will expect to be transformed by the renewing of our mind, to reset ourselves, to understand our context, to know God's design for families, to comprehend the future we will live in, and to serve in such a way to provide hope for children, families, and seniors with real-time solutions.

Family means you are never alone.

Families have the power to inspire hope today and in the future.

ABOUT BUCKNER INTERNATIONAL

Who We Are

Buckner International is a Christian ministry dedicated to following the example of Jesus by serving vulnerable children, families, and seniors. We protect children, strengthen families, and transform generations. As senior adults reach the sunset of life, we serve them to inspire happiness.

Why We Serve

We are driven by the teaching in James 1:27, "Religion that God our Father accepts as pure and faultless is this: to look after orphans and widows in their distress and to keep oneself from being polluted by the world." We follow Jesus into the villages, the communities, and the cities where the most vulnerable live. We shine the hope that is found in Christ. We inspire happiness among seniors in senior living communities. We seek to collaborate with government agencies, churches, and volunteers in the USA and abroad.

How We Serve

Our mission is "to follow the example of Jesus by serving vulnerable children, families, and seniors." Our vision is "to set the standard of excellence in serving vulnerable children, families, and seniors." Founded in 1879, we are the oldest children's charity in Dallas, focusing our work among vulnerable children, orphans, families, and seniors. We provide three major services among children: Foster Care and Adoption, Family Pathways, and Family Hope

Centers. We also provide foster care and adoptive services and support internationally. Family Pathways is a program serving single mothers with children to gain independence and economic sustainability in collaboration with colleges and universities to equip them for vocation and family health. Family Hope Centers are places where struggling families are strengthened and supported from a strengths-based model featuring protective factors all families need to succeed. We serve seniors in communities featuring independent living assisted living, skilled nursing, and memory care at six locations in Texas.

How You Can Help

Partnering with Buckner International provides tangible ways to bring the kingdom of God near, to shine hope, to bring peace, healing, and justice to those we serve. We need volunteers to serve children and families. You may wish to volunteer in your community, conduct a shoe drive, sort shoes, deliver shoes, or contribute financially through our programs. Together, with your support, we can make a difference for children, families, and seniors. To find out more about how you can help, visit www.buckner.org.

ACKNOWLEDGMENTS

Writing a book is a labor of love shared not only by the writer but by his family too. It was a family affair. My family has had to endure me talking about the lessons I was learning from the families of the Bible. They were my first audience. I have enjoyed the support of Dr. Belinda Reyes, my wife, and our adult sons. Thanks for your encouragement and for listening to me talk about this book and for providing feedback.

The Buckner International board of trustees patiently awaited the publication of this book. They supported me while I was leading Buckner International over the past three years. I wish to thank them for encouraging me to finish this book. I am indebted to the guidance of Dr. E. David Cook while writing this book. He is the founder of the Whitfield Institute in Oxford, England. Dr. Cook has continued to provide essential feedback and influence to produce the best possible manuscript I could write on this topic.

Leading Buckner International is an all-encompassing endeavor not meant for the faint of heart. Serving over 100,000 children, families, and seniors through 1,400 staff in Texas and 1,000 affiliated nongovernment organization staff in six countries requires the best of leadership. I cannot do this work alone. I am accompanied by an incredible dream team of professionals such as Arnie Adkison, who serves as senior vice president and chief development officer of the impact advancement team, and Scott Collins, senior vice president of the communications team, who both focus on external matters.

Renee Reimer, senior vice president and general counsel; Jeff Gentry, senior vice president of administration and chief financial officer, who leads our financial, information technology, facilities, and people operations teams; Jen Mann, our newest executive leader, serves as chief human resource officer and supports all we do through our incredible colleagues and associates; Kandyce Ormes Ripley, associate vice president of data analysis and strategy all provide internal support for Buckner ministry. Charlie Wilson, president of Buckner Retirement Services, Inc., and Henry Jackson, president of Buckner Children and Family Services, Inc., provide leadership for the two operational units that comprise the core Buckner ministry. Each of these senior leaders is supported by other teams of amazing leaders as well. I am grateful for their support, and I am hopeful this volume will add value to their families.

This book became a reality because of the effort of Julie Grabeel, senior executive assistant. Julie did an amazing job of helping me manage my day job while also making room for me to write. Managing my calendar was an art she mastered during this project. Any writing I was able to do was supported by the outstanding efforts of Michelle Volk, executive research consultant. Michelle paid immaculate attention to detail, gathered valuable documents, and produced amazing resources for me to use. Julie and Michelle were extremely helpful in compiling all the support documents at the end of this project. I am deeply grateful for their efforts, availability, attentiveness, and for following me in this adventure.

NOTES

Introduction: A Future Without a Family

1. Edward E. Hale, *The Man Without a Country and Other Tales* (Boston: Roberts Brothers, 1891), 13.
2. "The Man Without a Country," Wikipedia, https://en.wikipedia.org /wiki/The_Man_Without_a_Country.
3. Leonard I. Sweet, "Feb 10, 2017—Leonard Sweet," PLNU Chapel, February 13, 2017, https://www.youtube.com/watch?v= r4hkKIeFOPE.
4. Plato, *The Republic: Book V*, Webster's Thesaurus Edition (San Diego: Icon Classics, 2005), 425.
5. Plato, *Republic*, 429.
6. Plato, *Republic*, 435.
7. Richard Weikart, "Marx, Engels, and the Abolition of the Family," *History of European Ideas* 18, no. 5 (1994): 657–58, https://www .csustan.edu/sites/default/files/History/Faculty/Weikart/Marx -Engels-and-the-Abolition-of-the-Family.pdf.
8. "Oneida Community (1848–1880): A Utopian Community," VCU Libraries Social Welfare History Project, June 2017, http:// socialwelfare.library.vcu.edu/religous/the-oneida-community-1848 -1880-a-utopian-community/.
9. "Oneida Community (1848–1880)."
10. "Oneida Community (1848–1880)."
11. Melford E. Spiro, "Is the Family Universal?" *American Anthropologist* 56, no. 5, part 1 (October 1954): 839–46, https://doi.org/10.1525 /aa.1954.56.5.02a00080.
12. Spiro, "Is the Family Universal?" 839.
13. Spiro, "Is the Family Universal?" 840–42.

14. Lee Cronk, *That Complex Whole: Culture and the Evolution of Human Behavior* (New York: Routledge, 1999), 31.

15. Elizabeth Elizalde, "NYC School Encourages Kids to Stop Using Words like 'Mom,' 'Dad,' in 'Inclusive Language Guide,'" *New York Post*, March 10, 2021, http://www.nypost.com/2021/03/10/nyc-school -encourages-kids-to-stop-using-words-mom-dad/.

16. Elizalde, "NYC School Encourages Kids."

17. Véronique Munoz-Dardé, "Is the Family to Be Abolished Then?" *Proceedings of the Aristotelian Society* 99 (1999): 37–56, http://www.jstor .org/stable/4545294.

1. Design for Humanity

1. Torley Wong, "Behind the Design: 5 Stories of Great Inspiration," *Smashing Magazine*, October 1, 2008, https://www.smashingmagazine .com/2008/10/behind-the-design-5-stories-of-great-inspiration/.

2. "The Gardens: The Art of Perspective," Chateau de Versailles, https://en.chateauversailles.fr/discover/estate/gardens.

3. "About," Seaside, https://seasidefl.com/about#timeline.

4. "About," Seaside.

5. "About," Seaside.

6. "About," Seaside, see under "Explore Seaside Architecture."

7. Genesis 4:17–26; Genesis 5; Genesis 10; Genesis 36; Genesis 46:5– 26; Numbers 1; Numbers 34:16–29; 1 Chronicles 1; 1 Chronicles 2; 1 Chronicles 3; 1 Chronicles 4–9; 1 Chronicles 12:23–38; and Matthew 1:1–17.

8. Jim Denison, "'The Nuclear Family Was a Mistake': My Response to an Article of Seismic Significance," Denison Forum, February 13, 2020, https://www.denisonforum.org/daily-article/the-nuclear-family-was -a-mistake-my-response-to-an-article-of-seismic-significance/.

9. L. Murray and M. Barnes, "Have Families Been Rethought? Ethic of Care, Family and 'Whole Family' Approaches," *Social Policy and Society* 9, no. 4 (September 4, 2010): 533–44.

10. Mitchell Sviridoff and William Ryan, "Community-Centered Family Service," *Families in Society* 78, no. 2 (March-April 1997): 128–33, 138–39.

11. J. Laird, "Family-Centered Practice in the Post-Modern Era," *Families in Society* 76, no. 3 (March 1995): 150.

12. Suzanne Dixon, *The Roman Family* (Baltimore: Johns Hopkins University Press, 1992), 3.

13. Dixon, *Roman Family*, 29.

14. Stevan Harrell, *Human Families* (New York: Routledge, 2018), 552–53.

15. Inter-American Commission on Human Rights, "The Right of Girls and Boys to a Family. Alternative Care. Ending Institutionalization in the Americas." Organization of American States (October 17, 2013): 17, https://www.oas.org/en/iachr/reports/pdfs/Report-Right-to-family.doc.

16. Brad Wilcox and Hal Boyd, "The Nuclear Family Is Still Indispensable," *The Atlantic*, February 21, 2020, https://www.theatlantic.com/ideas/archive/2020/02/nuclear-family-still-indispensable/606841/.

17. Wilcox and Boyd, "Nuclear Family."

18. Wilcox and Boyd, "Nuclear Family."

19. Kurt Jefferson, "The American Family: The Stabilizing Factor in a Changing Society," Daily Life Through History, 2020, ABC-CLIO.

20. Brent Waters, *The Family in Christian Social and Political Thought* (Oxford, England: Oxford University Press, 2007), 9.

21. Waters, *Family in Christian Social and Political Thought*, 204.

2. The Divine Family

1. J. Paul Sampley, Joseph Burgess, Gerhard Krodel, and Reginald H. Fuller, *Ephesians, Colossians, 2 Thessalonians, The Pastoral Epistles*, The Proclamation Series: The New Testament Witnesses for Preaching, ed. Gerhard Krodel (Philadelphia: Fortress, 1978), 49–55.

2. David E. Garland, *Colossians/Philemon: The NIV Application Commentary* (Grand Rapids, MI: Zondervan, 1998), 87.

3. Kenneth L. Barker and John Kohlenberger III, *New Testament*, vol. 2, Zondervan NIV Bible Commentary (Grand Rapids, MI: Zondervan, 1994), 819.

4. Richard R. Melick, Jr., *Philippians, Colossians, Philemon*, vol. 32, New American Commentary (Nashville: Broadman, 1991), 214.

5. Garland, *Colossians/Philemon*, 87.

6. Scot McKnight, *The Letter to the Colossians*, The New International Commentary on the New Testament (Grand Rapids, MI: Eerdmans, 2018), 147.

7. G. K. Beale, *Colossians and Philemon*, Baker Exegetical Commentary on the New Testament (Grand Rapids, MI: Baker Academic, 2019), 81–84, 95.

8. Melick, *Philippians, Colossians, Philemon*, 217.

9. David M. Hay, *Colossians*, Abingdon New Testament Commentaries (Nashville: Abingdon, 2000), 62–65.

10. Andreas J. Köstenberger, *John*, Baker Exegetical Commentary on the New Testament (Grand Rapids, MI: Baker Academic, 2004), 304.

11. Margaret Aymer, Cynthia Briggs Kittredge, and David A. Sánchez, eds., *The Gospels and Acts*, Fortress Commentary on the Bible Study Edition (Minneapolis: Fortress, 2016), 287.

12. George Cladis, *Leading the Team-Based Church: How Pastors and Church Staffs Can Grow Together into a Powerful Fellowship of Leaders* (San Francisco: Josey-Bass, 1999), 4.

13. Cladis, *Leading the Team-Based Church*.

14. Millard J. Erickson, *Christian Theology* (Grand Rapids, MI: Baker, 1985), 342.

3. The First Family

1. Dietrich Bonhoeffer, *Creation and Fall: A Theological Exposition of Genesis 1–3*, vol. 3, Dietrich Bonhoeffer Works (Minneapolis: Fortress, 1997), 28.

2. John H. Sailhamer et al., *Genesis, Exodus, Leviticus, Numbers*, vol. 2, The Expositor's Bible Commentary, ed. Frank E. Gaebelein (Grand Rapids, MI: Zondervan, 1990), 60.

3. Victor P. Hamilton, *The Book of Genesis: Chapters 1–17*, The New International Commentary on the Old Testament (Grand Rapids, MI: Eerdmans, 1990), 220.

4. Hamilton, *Book of Genesis: Chapters 1–17*, 220.

5. Kenneth A. Mathews, *Genesis 1–11:26*, vol. 1A, The New American Commentary (Nashville: Broadman and Holman, 1996), 265.

6. Hamilton, *Book of Genesis: Chapters 1–17*, 222.

7. Hamilton, *Book of Genesis: Chapters 1–17*.

8. Hamilton, *Book of Genesis: Chapters 1–17*, 223.

9. Gordon J. Wenham, *Genesis 1–15*, vol. 1, Word Biblical Commentary (Waco: Word Books, 1987), 104.

10. Wenham, *Genesis 1–15*, 103.

11. Wenham, *Genesis 1–15*.

12. Wenham, *Genesis 1–15*, 104.

13. Mathews, *Genesis 1–11:26*, 268.

14. Hamilton, *Book of Genesis: Chapters 1–17*, 223.

15. Gerhard Von Rad, *Genesis: A Commentary*, rev. ed. (Philadelphia: Westminster, 1972), 103.

16. Von Rad, *Genesis*, 105.

17. Von Rad, *Genesis*.

18. Hamilton, *Book of Genesis: Chapters 1–17*, 226.

19. Hamilton, *Book of Genesis: Chapters 1–17*.

20. Wenham, *Genesis 1–15*, 106.

21. Wenham, *Genesis 1–15*, 105.

22. Hamilton, *Book of Genesis: Chapters 1–17*, 230.

23. Albertus Pieters, *Notes on Genesis: For Ministers and Serious Bible Students* (Grand Rapids, MI: Eerdmans, 1943), 104.

24. Wenham, *Genesis 1–15*, 106.

25. Wenham, *Genesis 1–15*.

26. Hamilton, *Book of Genesis: Chapters 1–17*, 231.

27. Wenham, *Genesis 1–15*, 107.

28. Wenham, *Genesis 1–15*.

29. Hamilton, *Book of Genesis: Chapters 1–17*, 231.

30. Wenham, *Genesis 1–15*, 107.

31. Von Rad, *Genesis*, 106.

32. Gale A. Yee, Hugh R. Page Jr., and Matthew J. M. Coomber, eds., *The Old Testament and Apocrypha*, Fortress Commentary on the Bible (Minneapolis: Fortress, 2014), 94.
33. Wenham, *Genesis 1–15*, 107.
34. Hamilton, *Book of Genesis: Chapters 1–17*, 232.
35. Hamilton, *Book of Genesis: Chapters 1–17*, 233.
36. Wenham, *Genesis 1–15*, 108–10.
37. Von Rad, *Genesis*, 107.
38. Hamilton, *Book of Genesis: Chapters 1–17*, 234.
39. Hamilton, *Book of Genesis: Chapters 1–17*, 235.
40. Jim Denison, "Where Did Cain Get His Wife?" Denison Forum, February 1, 2020, https://www.denisonforum.org/resources/where-did-cain-get-his-wife/.
41. Georgia Purdom, "Where Did Cain Get His Wife?" Answers in Genesis, July 1, 2014, https://answersingenesis.org/bible-characters/cain/creation-basics/.
42. Sailhamer et al., *Genesis, Exodus, Leviticus, Numbers*, 62.
43. Sailhamer et al., *Genesis, Exodus, Leviticus, Numbers*, 60.
44. Yee et al., *Old Testament and Apocrypha*, 96.
45. Thomas O. Chisolm, "Great Is Thy Faithfulness," Hymnary.org, https://hymnary.org/text/great_is_thy_faithfulness_o_god_my_fathe.

4. The Promised Family: Abraham

1. Albertus Pieters, *Notes on Genesis: For Ministers and Serious Bible Students* (Grand Rapids, MI: Eerdmans, 1943), 139.
2. John H. Sailhamer et al., *Genesis, Exodus, Leviticus, Numbers*, vol. 2 of The Expositor's Bible Commentary, ed. Frank E. Gaebelein (Grand Rapids, MI: Zondervan, 1990), 111.
3. Sailhamer et al., *Genesis, Exodus, Leviticus, Numbers*.
4. John H. Marks et al., *The Pentateuch: A Commentary on Genesis, Exodus, Leviticus, Numbers, Deuteronomy*, Interpreter's Concise Commentary, ed. Charles M. Laymon (Nashville: Abingdon, 1971), 30.
5. Pieters, *Notes on Genesis*, 139.

6. Sailhamer et al., *Genesis, Exodus, Leviticus, Numbers*, 112.

7. Kenneth A. Mathews, *Genesis 11:27–50:26*, vol. 1B, The New American Commentary (Nashville: Broadman Holman, 2005), 105.

8. Gordon J. Wenham, *Genesis 1–15*, vol. 1, Word Biblical Commentary (Waco: Word Books, 1987), 274.

9. Wenham, *Genesis 1–15*.

10. Mathews, *Genesis 11:27–50:26*, 109.

11. Victor P. Hamilton, *The Book of Genesis: Chapters 1–17*, The New International Commentary on the Old Testament (Grand Rapids, MI: Eerdmans, 1990), 371.

12. Mathews, *Genesis 11:27–50:26*, 113.

13. Wenham, *Genesis 1–15*, 275.

14. Gerhard Von Rad, *Genesis: A Commentary* (Philadelphia: Westminster, 1972), 160.

15. Von Rad, *Genesis*.

16. Mathews, *Genesis 11:27–50:26*, 114.

17. Wenham, *Genesis 1–15*, 275.

18. Mathews, *Genesis 11:27–50:26*, 115.

19. Hamilton, *Book of Genesis: Chapters 1–17*, 373.

20. Hamilton, *Book of Genesis: Chapters 1–17*, 374.

21. Mathews, *Genesis 11:27–50:26*, 118.

22. Marcus Dods, *The Book of Genesis* (New York: A. C. Armstrong & Son, 1902), 136.

23. John Skinner, *A Critical and Exegetical Commentary on Genesis* (Edinburgh, Scotland: T & T Clark, 1994), 279.

24. Wenham, *Genesis 1–15*, 327.

25. Hamilton, *Book of Genesis: Chapters 1–17*, 418.

26. Hamilton, *Book of Genesis: Chapters 1–17*, 418.

27. Wenham, *Genesis 1–15*, 327.

28. Hamilton, *Book of Genesis: Chapters 1–17*, 419.

29. Hamilton, *Book of Genesis: Chapters 1–17*, 418.

30. Sailhamer et al., *Genesis, Exodus, Leviticus, Numbers*, 127.

31 Wenham, *Genesis 1–15*, 329.

32. Mathews, *Genesis 11:27–50:26*, 165.

33. Mathews, *Genesis 11:27–50:26*, 166.

34. Pieters, *Notes on Genesis*, 145.

35. Wenham, *Genesis 1–15*, 329.

36. Pieters, *Notes on Genesis*, 147.

37. Marks et al., *Pentateuch*, 41.

38. Pieters, *Notes on Genesis*, 147.

39. Skinner, *Critical and Exegetical Commentary*, 284.

40. Hamilton, *Book of Genesis: Chapters 1–17*, 443.

41. Sailhamer et al., *Genesis, Exodus, Leviticus, Numbers*, 135.

42. Von Rad, *Genesis*, 191.

43. Hamilton, *Book of Genesis: Chapters 1–17*, 444.

44. Mathews, *Genesis 11:27–50:26*, 185.

45. Hamilton, *Book of Genesis: Chapters 1–17*, 446.

46. Sailhamer et al., *Genesis, Exodus, Leviticus, Numbers*, 135.

47. Mathews, *Genesis 11:27–50:26*, 184.

48. Mathews, *Genesis 11:27–50:26*, 185.

49. Dods, *Book of Genesis*, 151.

50. Pieters, *Notes on Genesis*, 147.

51. Pieters, *Notes on Genesis*, 148.

52. Dods, *Book of Genesis*, 151.

53. Hamilton, *Book of Genesis: Chapters 1–17*, 446.

54. Skinner, *Critical and Exegetical Commentary*, 286.

55. Mathews, *Genesis 11:27–50:26*, 182.

56. Mathews, *Genesis 11:27–50:26*, 178.

57. Dods, *Book of Genesis*, 147.

58. Mathews, *Genesis 11:27–50:26*, 182.

59. Marks, *Pentateuch*, 41.

60. Pieters, *Notes on Genesis*, 148.

61. Pieters, *Notes on Genesis*.

62. Mathews, *Genesis 11:27–50:26*, 179.

63. Pieters, *Notes on Genesis*, 148.

64. Dods, *Book of Genesis*, 154.

65. Pieters, *Notes on Genesis*, 148.

66. Dods, *Book of Genesis*, 159.

67. Marks, *Pentateuch*, 42.

68. Mathews, *Genesis 11:27–50:26*, 201.

69. Pieters, *Notes on Genesis*, 149.

70. Marks, *Pentateuch*, 43.

71. Marks, *Pentateuch*.

72. Sailhamer et al., *Genesis, Exodus, Leviticus, Numbers*, 138–39.

73. Hamilton, *Book of Genesis: Chapters 1–17*, 463.

74. Hamilton, *Book of Genesis: Chapters 1–17*, 464.

75. Sailhamer et al., *Genesis, Exodus, Leviticus, Numbers*, 139.

76. Hamilton, *Book of Genesis: Chapters 1–17*, 465.

77. Dods, *Book of Genesis*, 168.

78. Dods, *Book of Genesis*, 171.

79. Dods, *Book of Genesis*.

5. The Promised Family: Isaac

1. John H. Sailhamer et al., *Genesis, Exodus, Leviticus, Numbers*, vol. 2, The Expositor's Bible Commentary, ed. Frank E. Gaebelein (Grand Rapids, MI: Zondervan, 1990), 168.

2. Albertus Pieters, *Notes on Genesis: For Ministers and Serious Bible Students* (Grand Rapids, MI: Eerdmans, 1943), 157.

3. Pieters, *Notes on Genesis*, 158.

4. Sailhamer et al., *Genesis, Exodus, Leviticus, Numbers*, 168.

5. Sailhamer et al., *Genesis, Exodus, Leviticus, Numbers*, 168.

6. Kenneth A. Mathews, *Genesis 1–11:26*, vol. 1A, The New American Commentary (Nashville: Broadman and Holman, 1996), 295.

7. Marcus Dods, *The Book of Genesis* (New York: A. C. Armstrong & Son, 1902), 201.

8. Dods, *Book of Genesis*, 205–6.

9. John Skinner, *A Critical and Exegetical Commentary on Genesis* (Edinburgh, Scotland: T & T Clark, 1994), 330.

10. Dods, *Book of Genesis*, 208–9.

11. Richard Oxenburg, "The Teleological Suspension of the Ethical: Abraham, Isaac, and the Challenge of Faith," PhilArchive, 2018, https://philarchive.org/archive/OXETTS.

12. Mathews, *Genesis 1–11:26*, 355.

13. Gerhard Von Rad, *Genesis: A Commentary*, rev. ed. (Philadelphia: Westminster, 1972), 262.

14. John H. Marks et al., *The Pentateuch: A Commentary on Genesis, Exodus, Leviticus, Numbers, Deuteronomy*, Interpreter's Concise Commentary, ed. Charles M. Laymon (Nashville: Abingdon, 1971), 55.

15. Sailhamer et al., *Genesis, Exodus, Leviticus, Numbers*, 182.

16. Von Rad, *Genesis*, 264.

17. Victor P. Hamilton, *The Book of Genesis: Chapters 18–50*, The New International Commentary on the Old Testament (Grand Rapids, MI: Eerdmans, 1990), 177.

18. Dods, *Book of Genesis*, 256.

19. Hamilton, *Book of Genesis: Chapters 18–50*, 181.

20. Mathews, *Genesis 1–11:26*, 391.

21. Sailhamer et al., *Genesis, Exodus, Leviticus, Numbers*, 182.

22. Mathews, *Genesis 1–11:26*, 388.

23. Mathews, *Genesis 1–11:26*, 391.

24. Mathews, *Genesis 1–11:26*, 387–88.

25. Sailhamer et al., *Genesis, Exodus, Leviticus, Numbers*, 182–83.

26. Marks et al., *Pentateuch*, 56.

27 Mathews, *Genesis 1–11:26*, 393.

28. Skinner, *Critical and Exegetical Commentary on Genesis*, 362.

29. Sailhamer et al., *Genesis, Exodus, Leviticus, Numbers*, 183.

30. Mathews, *Genesis 1–11:26*, 392.

31. Hamilton, *Book of Genesis: Chapters 18–50*, 182.

32. Pieters, *Notes on Genesis*, 162.

33. Hamilton, *Book of Genesis: Chapters 18–50*, 183.

34. Pieters, *Notes on Genesis*, 162.

35. Hamilton, *Book of Genesis: Chapters 18–50*, 186.

36. Dods, *Book of Genesis*, 264.

37. Mathews, *Genesis 1–11:26*, 417.

38. Marks et al., *Pentateuch*, 57.

39. Mathews, *Genesis 1–11:26*, 417.

40. Mathews, *Genesis 1–11:26*.

41. Marks et al., *Pentateuch*, 57.

42. Dods, *Book of Genesis*, 271.

43. Mathews, *Genesis 1–11:26*, 423.

44. Dods, *Book of Genesis*, 274.

45. Matthews, *Genesis 1–11:26*, 437.

46. Von Rad, *Genesis*, 279.

47. Dods, *Book of Genesis*, 278.

48. Dods, *Book of Genesis*.

49. Dods, *Book of Genesis*, 158.

6. The Redeeming Family

1. Gale A. Yee, Hugh R. Page Jr., and Matthew J. M. Coomber, eds., *The Old Testament and Apocrypha*, Fortress Commentary on the Bible (Minneapolis: Fortress, 2014), 128.

2. Yee et al., *Old Testament and Apocrypha*.

3. Victor P. Hamilton, *The Book of Genesis: Chapters 18–50*, The New International Commentary on the Old Testament (Grand Rapids, MI: Eerdmans, 1995), 702.

4. Kenneth A. Mathews, *Genesis 11:27–50:26*, vol. 1B, The New American Commentary (Nashville: Broadman Holman, 2005), 921.

5. Gerhard Von Rad, *Genesis: A Commentary*, rev. ed. (Philadelphia: Westminster, 1972), 431.

6. Yee et al., *Old Testament and Apocrypha*, 131.

7. Hamilton, *Book of Genesis: Chapters 18–50*, 704–5.

8. Mathews, *Genesis 11:27–50:26*, 921.

9. Hamilton, *Book of Genesis: Chapters 18–50*, 707.

10. Von Rad, *Genesis*, 432.

11. John H. Sailhamer et al., *Genesis, Exodus, Leviticus, Numbers*, vol. 2, The Expositor's Bible Commentary, ed. Frank E. Gaebelein (Grand Rapids, MI: Zondervan, 1990), 283.

12. John H. Marks et al., *The Pentateuch: A Commentary of Genesis, Exodus, Leviticus, Numbers, and Deuteronomy*, Interpreter's Concise Commentary, ed. Charles M. Laymon (Nashville: Abingdon, 1971), 88.

13. Yee et al., *Old Testament and Apocrypha*, 131–32.

14. Mathews, *Genesis 11:27–50:26*, 922.

15. Yee et al., *Old Testament and Apocrypha*, 132.

16. Yee et al., *Old Testament and Apocrypha*, 134.

7. The Liberating Family

1. Douglas K. Stuart, *Exodus*, vol. 2 of The New American Commentary (Nashville: Broadman & Holman, 2006), 85.

2. William H. C. Propp, *Exodus 1–18*, The Anchor Yale Bible Commentaries (New York: Doubleday, 1999), 149.

3. Stuart, *Exodus*, 87–88.

4. John I. Durham, *Exodus*, vol. 3, Word Biblical Commentary (Waco: Word, 1987), 16.

5. Propp, *Exodus 1–18*, 149.

6. Terence E. Fretheim, *Exodus*, Interpretation: A Bible Commentary for Teaching and Preaching (Louisville: John Knox, 1991), 36–37.

7. Stuart, *Exodus*, 87.

8. Stuart, *Exodus*, 90.

9. John H. Sailhamer et al., *Genesis, Exodus, Leviticus, Numbers*, vol. 2, The Expositor's Bible Commentary, ed. Frank E. Gaebelein (Grand Rapids, MI: Zondervan, 1990), 309.

10. Durham, *Exodus*, 16.

11. Sailhamer et al., *Genesis, Exodus, Leviticus, Numbers*, 309.

12. Stuart, *Exodus*, 91–92.

13. Durham, *Exodus*, 16.

14. Stuart, *Exodus*, 89.

15. Stuart, *Exodus*, 92.

16. Durham, *Exodus*, 16.

17. Durham, *Exodus*, 17.

18. Lester Meyer, *The Message of Exodus: A Theological Commentary* (Minneapolis: Augsburg, 1983), 37.

19. Stuart, *Exodus*, 93.

20. Stuart, *Exodus*, 93.

21. Stuart, *Exodus*, 85.

22. Fretheim, *Exodus*, 39.

23. Michael V. Fox, *Proverbs 10–31*, The Anchor Yale Bible Commentaries (New Haven, CT: Yale University Press, 2009), 894.

24. Bruce K. Waltke, *The Book of Proverbs: Chapters 15–31*, The New International Commentary on the Old Testament (Grand Rapids, MI: Eerdmans, 2005), 524.

25. Fox, *Proverbs 10–31*, 912.

26. Roland Murphy, *Proverbs*, vol. 22, Word Biblical Commentary (Nashville: Thomas Nelson, 1998), 245.

27. Murphy, *Proverbs*.

28. Waltke, *Book of Proverbs: Chapters 15–31*, 525.

29. Fox, *Proverbs 10–31*, 890.

30. Waltke, *Book of Proverbs: Chapters 15–31*, 532.

31. Murphy, *Proverbs*, 245–46.

32. Ernest C. Lucas, *Proverbs*, The Two Horizons Old Testament Commentary (Grand Rapids, MI: Eerdmans, 2015), 196.

33. Milton P. Horne, *Proverbs-Ecclesiastes*, Smyth & Helwys Bible Commentary (Macon, GA: Smyth & Helwys, 2003), 365.

34. R. F. Horton, *The Expositor's Bible: The Book of Proverbs* (New York: A. C. Armstrong & Son, 1908), 398.

35. Horton, *Book of Proverbs*, 399.

36. Horton, *Book of Proverbs*, 409.

8. The Royal Family

1. Gale A. Yee, Hugh R. Page Jr., and Matthew J. M. Coomber, *The Old Testament and Apocrypha*, Fortress Commentary on the Bible (Minneapolis: Fortress, 2014), 393.

2. P. Kyle McCarter Jr., *II Samuel*, The Anchor Yale Bible Commentaries (Garden City, NY: Doubleday, 1984), 405.

3. Walter Brueggemann, *First and Second Samuel*, Interpretation: A Bible Commentary for Teaching and Preaching (Louisville: John Knox, 1990), 317.

4. Yee et al., *Old Testament and Apocrypha*, 392.

5. Brueggemann, *First and Second Samuel*, 319.

6. Robert D. Bergen, *1, 2 Samuel*, The New American Commentary (Nashville: Broadman & Holman, 1996), 421.

7. Hans Wilhelm Hertzberg, *I & II Samuel*, The Old Testament Library (Philadelphia: Westminster, 1964), 359.

8. Henry Preserved Smith, *A Critical and Exegetical Commentary on the Books of Samuel* (New York: Charles Scribner's Sons, 1899), 361.

9. John H. Sailhamer et al., *Genesis, Exodus, Leviticus, Numbers*, vol. 2, The Expositor's Bible Commentary, ed. Frank E. Gaebelein (Grand Rapids, MI: Zondervan, 1990), 1020.

10. McCarter, *II Samuel*, 407.

11. W. G. Blaikie, *The Expositor's Bible: The Second Book of Samuel* (New York: A. C. Armstrong and Son, 1908), 274.

12. Blaikie, *Second Book of Samuel*, 274–75.

13. McCarter, *II Samuel*, 411.

14. Sailhamer et al., *Genesis, Exodus, Leviticus, Numbers*, 1028.

15. Blaikie, *Second Book of Samuel*, 281–82.

16. A. A. Anderson, *2 Samuel*, vol. 11, Word Biblical Commentary (Dallas: Word, 1989), 228.

17. Brueggemann, *First and Second Samuel*, 322–23.

18. McCarter, *II Samuel*, 409.

19. Blaikie, *Second Book of Samuel*, 282.

20. Tony W. Cartledge, *1 & 2 Samuel*, Smyth & Helwys Bible Commentary (Macon, GA: Smyth & Helwys, 2001), 608.

21. Blaikie, *Second Book of Samuel*, 282–83.

22. Blaikie, *Second Book of Samuel*, 283.

23. Yee et al., *Old Testament and Apocrypha*, 394.

24. For an excellent tool to develop healthy relationships with teenagers, see Dr. Richard Ross and Dr. Gus Reyes, *30 Days: Turning the Hearts of Parents and Teenagers Toward Each Other* (Nashville: Lifeway, 2007).

9. The Holy Family

1. John Nolland, *Luke 1–9:20*, vol. 35A of Word Biblical Commentary (Dallas: Word, 1989), 105.

2. Darrell L. Bock, *Luke*, The NIV Application Commentary (Grand Rapids, MI: Zondervan, 1996), 92.

3. Fred B. Craddock, *Luke*, Interpretation: A Bible Commentary for Teaching and Preaching (Louisville: John Knox, 1990), 41.

4. D. B. J. Campbell, *The Synoptic Gospels: A Commentary for Teachers and Students* (New York: Seabury, 1966), 21–22.

5. F. Scott Spencer, *Luke*, The Two Horizons New Testament Commentary (Grand Rapids, MI: Eerdmans, 2019), 79.

6. Nolland, *Luke 1–9:20*, 134.

7. J. R. H. Moorman, *The Path to Glory: Studies in the Gospel According to Saint Luke* (London: Society for Promoting Christian Knowledge, 1960), 28.

8. Alfred Plummer, *A Critical and Exegetical Commentary on the Gospel According to St. Luke* (New York: Charles Scribner's Sons, 1902), 75.

9. Robert C. Tannehill, *Luke*, Abingdon New Testament Commentaries (Nashville: Abingdon, 1996), 75.

10. Spencer, *Luke*, 79.

11. Nolland, *Luke 1–9:20*, 130.

12. Bock, *Luke*, 100.

13. Richard Vinson, *Luke*, Smith & Helwys Bible Commentary (Macon, GA: Smyth & Helwys, 2008), 77.

14. Spencer, *Luke*, 82–83.

15. Spencer, *Luke*, 83.

16. Norval Geldenhuys, *Commentary on the Gospel of Luke: The English Text with Introduction, Exposition, and Notes* (Grand Rapids, MI: Eerdmans, 1988), 127–28.

17. Tannehill, *Luke*, 77.

18. Moorman, *Path to Glory*, 29.

19. Nolland, *Luke 1–9:20*, 134

20. Joseph A. Fitzmyer, *The Gospel According to Luke I-IX*, The Anchor Bible (Garden City, NY: Doubleday, 1981), 439.

21. William F. Arndt, *Luke*, Concordia Classic Commentary Series (St. Louis: Concordia, 1956), 102.

22. Tannehill, *Luke*, 75.

23. Nolland, *Luke 1–9:20*, 131.

24. Arndt, *Luke*, 98.

25. Spencer, *Luke*, 85.

26. Geldenhuys, *Commentary on the Gospel of Luke*, 129.

10. The Transformed Family

1. Albert L. Reyes, *The Jesus Agenda: Becoming an Agent of Redemption* (Nashville: Believers, 2015), 55.
2. Reyes, *Jesus Agenda*, 56.
3. A. T. Robertson, *Acts*, vol. 3, Word Pictures in the New Testament (Nashville: Broadman, 1930), 260.
4. Robertson, *Acts*, 260.
5. Robertson, *Acts*, 261.
6. Ajith Fernando, *Acts*, The NIV Application Commentary (Grand Rapids, MI: Zondervan, 1998), 446.
7. Fernando, *Acts*, 445.
8. J. Bradley Chance, *Acts*, Smith & Helwys Bible Commentary (Macon, GA: Smyth & Helwys, 2007), 290.
9. Robertson, *Acts*, 262.
10. Beverly Roberts Gaventa, *Acts*, Abingdon New Testament Commentaries (Nashville: Abingdon, 2003), 240.
11. I. Howard Marshall, *The Book of Acts: An Introduction and Commentary*, Tyndale New Testament Commentaries (Grand Rapids, MI; Cambridge, UK: Eerdmans, 1980), 273.
12. Darrell L. Bock, *Acts*, Baker Exegetical Commentary on the New Testament (Grand Rapids, MI: Baker Academic, 2007), 542.
13. Gaventa, *Acts*, 240.
14. Robertson, *Acts*, 265.

11. The Flourishing Family

1. Carle C. Zimmerman, *Family and Civilization* (New York: Harper & Brothers, 1947), 125–26, 130, 134.
2. Zimmerman, *Family and Civilization*, 238.
3. Zimmerman, *Family and Civilization*, 801.
4. Zimmerman, *Family and Civilization*, 806.
5. Thom Wolf, "Lifecode: An Examination of the Shape, the Nature, and the Usage of the Oikoscode, a Replicative Nonformal Learning Pattern of Ethical Education for Leadership and Community Groups"

(PhD diss., Andrews University, 2010), https://dx.doi.org/10.32597/dissertations/1555.

6. A. Skevington Wood et al., *Ephesians–Philemon*, vol. 11, The Expositor's Bible Commentary, ed. Frank E. Gaebelein (Grand Rapids, MI: Zondervan, 1978), 395.

7. William D. Mounce, *Pastoral Epistles*, vol. 46, Word Biblical Commentary (Nashville: Thomas Nelson, 2000), 471.

8. Thomas C. Oden, *First and Second Timothy and Titus*, Interpretation: A Bible Commentary for Teaching and Preaching (Louisville: John Knox, 1989), 29.

9. W. Hulitt Gloer, *1 & 2 Timothy–Titus*, Smith & Helwys Bible Commentary (Macon, GA: Smyth & Helwys, 2010), 221.

10. Gloer, *1 & 2 Timothy–Titus*, 221.

11. Gloer, *1 & 2 Timothy–Titus*.

12. Oden, *First and Second Timothy and Titus*, 28.

13. Gloer, *1 & 2 Timothy–Titus*, 221.

14. Mounce, *Pastoral Epistles*, 468.

15. Gloer, *1 & 2 Timothy–Titus*, 225–26.

16. Walter L. Liefeld, *1 & 2 Timothy, Titus*, The NIV Application Commentary (Grand Rapids, MI: Zondervan, 1999), 225.

17. Liefeld, *1 & 2 Timothy, Titus*, 228.

18. Oden, *First and Second Timothy and Titus*, 28–29.

19. Oden, *First and Second Timothy and Titus*, 29.

20. Oden, *First and Second Timothy and Titus*, 30.

21. Oden, *First and Second Timothy and Titus*.

22. Jouette M. Bassler, *1 Timothy, 2 Timothy, Titus*, Abingdon New Testament Commentaries (Nashville: Abingdon, 1996), 129.

23. Luke Timothy Johnson, *The First and Second Letters to Timothy*, The Anchor Yale Bible Commentaries (New York: Doubleday, 2001), 342.

24. Johnson, *First and Second Letters to Timothy*, 343.

25. Johnson, *First and Second Letters to Timothy*.

26. Wolf, "Lifecode," 19.

12. The Thriving Family

1. Russ Dilday, "How Did We Get There?" *Buckner Today* (Winter 2012): 30.

2. Albert L. Reyes, *Hope Now: Peace, Healing, and Justice When the Kingdom Comes Near* (Birmingham: Iron Stream, 2019), 134.

3. Dilday, "How Did We Get There?" 30.

4. Buckner International, *Move: The 2021 Buckner Annual Report*, 8.

5. Dilday, "How Did We Get There?" 29.

6. Dilday, "How Did We Get There?" 30.

7. Dilday, "How Did We Get There?"

8. See "About Strengthening Families and The Protective Factors Framework," Center for the Study of Social Policy, https://cssp.org/resource/about-strengthening-families-and-the-protective-factors-framework/.

9. For a holistic approach to community transformation, see Alexandra Rice, "A Purposeful Strategy Transforms Atlanta Neighborhood and Schools," *Education Week* 31, no. 3, 12–13.

10. "Buckner Family Hope Centers: Together We Can Keep Children and Families Intact," a Buckner Development Brochure (2016).

11. Kimberly Allen and Nichole L. Huff, "Family Coaching: An Emerging Family Science Field," *Family Relations, National Council on Family Relations* 63, no. 5 (December 2014): 569–82.

12. Allen and Huff, "Family Coaching."

13. Kathleen Strottman, "The State of Adoption," presented to the Buckner International Board, January 25, 2018.

14. Jedd Medefind, "The State of Child Welfare in the United States," presented to the Buckner International Board, January 24, 2019.

13. The Remade Family

1. James Britton Cranfill and J. L. Walker, *R. C. Buckner's Life of Faith and Works: Comprising the Story of the Career of the Preacher, Editor, Presiding Officer, Philanthropist, and Founder of Buckner Orphans Home*, 2nd ed. (Dallas: Buckner Orphans Home, 1996), 85–91.

2. Scott Collins, "Buckner Awarded USAID Grant for Work in Guatemala," Buckner, September 9, 2013, https://www.buckner.org/blog/buckner-awarded-usaid-grant-for-work-in-guatemala.

3. Collins, "Buckner Awarded USAID Grant."

4. Collins, "Buckner Awarded USAID Grant."

5. John Hall, "USAID Grant Progresses for Buckner Foster Care in Guatemala," Buckner, January 2, 2014, https://www.buckner.org /blog/usaid-grant-progresses-for-buckner-foster-care-in-guatemala.

6. Hall, "USAID Grant Progresses for Buckner Foster Care in Guatemala."

7. Scott Collins, "Lost and Found: Baby Sara's Joyful Return Home," Buckner, January 10, 2015, https://www.buckner.org/blog/lost-and -found-baby-saras-joyful-return-home.

8. Russ Dilday, "Gone: Kidnapped at Birth," Buckner, March 16, 2015, https://www.buckner.org/blog/gone-kidnapped-at-birth.

9. Lauren Sturdy, "Marked by Love: Bringing Valeria Home," Buckner, May 14, 2015, https://www.buckner.org/blog/marked-by-love -bringing-valeria-home.

10. Albert Reyes, "From the President: Buckner Nation," Buckner, May 28, 2015, https://www.buckner.org/blog/from-the-president-buckner -nation.

11. "Buckner International, Fostering Hope Guatemala: Finding Solutions for Children in Crisis," The Fostering Hope Guatemala Report 2013–2015.

12. Albert York, "Final Evaluation, USAID Grant," electronic communication, October 2015.

13. Reyes, "From the President: Buckner Nation."

14. See www.bebglobal.org for more information.

15. Thom Wolf, "Development and Its Implications for the Indian Social System: A WV3 Case Study of Jotirao Phule," *Comparative Civilizations Review* vol. 74, no. 74, article 4, (2016), https://scholarsarchive.byu .edu/ccr/vol74/iss74/4.

14. Family Hope

1. James Britton Cranfill and J. L. Walker, *R. C. Buckner's Life of Faith and Works: Comprising the Story of the Career of the Preacher, Editor, Presiding Officer, Philanthropist, and Founder of the Buckner Orphans Home*, 2nd ed. (Dallas, Texas: Buckner Orphans Home, 1996), 7–10.

2. Cranfill and Walker, *R. C. Buckner's Life of Faith and Works*, 26.

3. Cranfill and Walker, *R. C. Buckner's Life of Faith and Works*, 31.

4. Cranfill and Walker, *R. C. Buckner's Life of Faith and Works*, 35.

5. David Cross, telephone interview with author, April 27, 2023. Mr. Cross is the church historian of the First Baptist Church of Albany.

6. Cranfill and Walker, *R. C. Buckner's Life of Faith and Works*, 36–43.

7. Cranfill and Walker, *R. C. Buckner's Life of Faith and Works*, 43.

8. Cranfill and Walker, *R. C. Buckner's Life of Faith and Works*, 85–86.

9. Jerre Graves Simmons, ed., *Buckner Memoirs: The Orphan Chronicles* (Dallas: Nortex, 2000), vii.

10. Simmons, *Buckner Memoirs*.

11. Harry Leon McBeth, Texas Baptists: A Sesquicentennial History (Dallas: Baptistway, 1998), 138.

12. Karen O'Dell Bullock, *Homeward Bound: The Heart and Heritage of Buckner* (Dallas: Buckner International, 2009), 60.

13. Bullock, *Homeward Bound*, 100–129.

14. Bullock, *Homeward Bound*, 150.

15. Bullock, *Homeward Bound*, 160.

16. Bullock, *Homeward Bound*, 166–67.

17. Bullock, *Homeward Bound*, 207–38.

18. Paul Collier, *Exodus: How Migration Is Changing Our World* (New York: Oxford University Press, 2013), 11–16.

19. Stephen L. Klineberg, *Prophetic City: Houston on the Cusp of a Changing America* (New York: Simon and Schuster, 2020), 167.

20. Stephen Klineberg, "Prophetic City: Houston at the Cusp of a Changing America, Tracking Public Responses to the Economic and Demographic Transformations Through Forty-One Years of Survey Research" (paper presented at the Leadership Retreat at Buckner International, October 6, 2022).

21. Elijah Brown, "Six Winds of Change from the Future" (address to the Executive Council of the Baptist World Alliance, Falls Church, Virginia, March 7, 2023).

22. Mauro F. Guillén, *2030: How Today's Biggest Trends Will Collide and Reshape the Future of Everything* (New York: St. Martin's, 2020), 4–10.

23. Philip Jenkins, *The Next Christendom: The Coming of Global Christianity* (New York: Oxford University Press, 2002), 2–7.

Conclusion

1. Emma Wenner, "Rick Warren Brings a New Book to Zondervan," *Publisher's Weekly*, February 22, 2023, https://www.publishersweekly .com/pw/by-topic/industry-news/religion/article/91593-rick -warren-brings-a-new-book-to-zondervan.html.

ABOUT THE AUTHOR

Albert L. Reyes is the sixth president and CEO of Buckner International and a native of Corpus Christi, Texas. He became president of Buckner Children and Family Services, Inc., in 2007, president of Buckner International in 2010, and president and CEO of Buckner International in 2012. Prior to service at Buckner International, he served as the sixth president of Baptist University of the Américas. His leadership experience over the past thirty years includes telecom service management, military chaplaincy, pastoral ministry, university president, and executive leadership at Buckner International.

Albert earned a bachelor of business administration degree in management from Angelo State University, a master of divinity degree and doctor of ministry degree in missiology from Southwestern Baptist Theological Seminary, and a doctor of philosophy degree in leadership from Andrews University. He has participated in executive management at the Harvard Kennedy School of Government, and postdoctoral study at the Oxford Centre for Mission Studies in Oxford, England.

He served as president of the Baptist General Convention of Texas in 2004; vice president of the North American Baptist Fellowship, a regional fellowship of the Baptist World Alliance; and currently serves as vice president of the Baptist World Alliance representing Baptists in the United States of America. He serves on the boards of the Christian Alliance for Orphans, National Hispanic Christian Leadership Conference, and Stark College and Seminary.

He is the author of *The Jesus Agenda: Becoming an Agent of Redemption* and *Hope Now: Peace, Healing, and Justice When the Kingdom Comes Near*, both published in English and Spanish. Albert and his wife, Belinda, have three adult sons—Joshua, David, and Thomas—and are members of Park Cities Baptist Church in Dallas.